DEALING WITH BEHAVIORAL PROBLEMS IN THE ELEMENTARY SCHOOL

DEALING WITH BEHAVIORAL PROBLEMS IN THE ELEMENTARY SCHOOL

R. Warburton Miller

and

Joyce Larayne Miller

PARKER PUBLISHING COMPANY, INC.
West Nyack, N.Y.

LIBRARY OF CONGRESS
CATALOG CARD NUMBER: 69-19783

Fourth Printing.....March, 1972

PRINTED IN THE UNITED STATES OF AMERICA
13-197269-3 B & P

DEDICATION

This book is gratefully dedicated to: PAM, BRENT, and PAGE, our three children. They have continuously been able to give us "feedback," insight, and a fine perspective from their point of view. Much of our learning has come from them, and we are truly thankful.

GUIDELINES FOR
THE CLASSROOM TEACHER

This is a practical "how-to" book, written to help the elementary school teacher recognize, cope with, and give counsel concerning most of the emotionally-oriented problems that normal children may develop. Since they never occur all at once, and since there are so many, the teacher needs a ready source of reference to supply her with ideas, standards of behavior, and guidelines in counseling children with these various problems.

Like each of us, every child at times experiences difficulties in accepting, adjusting to and coping with himself, the people around him, and the environment in which he lives. In many instances, he is able to handle these problems. As he grows in experience and knowledge, his solutions become more effective and reflect greater maturity. Periodically, however, these problems may get out of hand.

So that he may grow, the child needs support and counsel. The processes of normal discipline, teaching, and positive interpersonal relationships tend to resolve most of these problems. On occasion, however, they become severe enough to require special attention, and this book will assist you, the elementary teacher, in counseling with this child, whom we call the "special case." He is still classified as normal. This "special case" may have neurotic symptoms, but is not so severely neurotic or psychotic that he is unable to function in the classroom and playground environment.

The material that follows is designed to help the elementary school teacher to:

1. Recognize the normal child who may be developing into a "special case," or who may already be one.
2. Establish procedures and develop techniques in counseling the child and in helping him to:
   a) Mature.
   b) Cope with the realities of the classroom and playground.

    c) Accept himself as he is with his potentials and limitations.

    d) Adjust to a society with controls, opportunities, and restrictions.

3. Carry out a realistic counseling program that will support and assist him as he attempts to:

    a) Resolve his problems.

    b) Find effective, socially acceptable outlets for his needs.

    c) Adopt techniques that tend to prevent the development of more neurotic actions.

    d) Return to acceptable behavior patterns.

4. Recognize possible neurotic and psychotic symptoms. When necessary, refer the child, with an adequate case history and supportive material, to specialists—either to the special services department of the school district or to the various public and private sources equipped to handle this child.

This book will offer specific guidelines for counseling the elementary school child from a directive, as well as a non-directive point of view. Carefully followed, these guidelines will help the individual teacher acquire experience and strengthen skills in *Dealing with Behavioral Problems in the Elementary School.*

ACKNOWLEDGMENTS

We gratefully acknowledge the helpfulness and insight provided by the following individuals, all professionals in the field of child behavior problems, and all in some way involved with school administration, special services departments, teaching, or private practice in mental health fields.

James E. Blanchette, M.D., F.A.P.C., Formerly Assistant Superintendent Psychiatric Services, Patton State Hospital; Private Practice, Clinical Assistant Professor Loma Linda University Medical School, California.

Walter C. Engel, M.D., General Practice, Colton, California.

Sarita M. Gillam, A.B., General Elementary Certificate, First Grade Teacher—Alvord Unified School District, Riverside, California.

Frederick C. Hammond, B.A., B.D., Vicar of St. George's Episcopal Church, El Toro, California.

Loretta F. Hancock, A.B., M.A. (in Special Education), Master Teacher (Trainable Mentally Retarded) San Bernardino County School Office, Magnolia School, Ontario, California.

Carol L. Harper, B.S., Credentialed in Elementary and Secondary School Systems in Texas, Virginia, Oklahoma, Ohio, and California; First Grade Teacher—Eliot Elementary School, San Bernardino City Unified School District, Cailfornia.

Lilbern Lynn Parker, A.B., B.D., Counselor for California Department of Correction at the California Rehabilitation Center (Narcotic), Norco, California.

Ruby Mitchell Parker, B.A.—Life Diploma in General Elementary Education—Ten years in Primary Grades, now teaching Educationally Handicapped, La Granada School, Alvord Unified School District, Riverside, California.

John A. Ragsdale, B.A., M.A., General Elementary Credential, General Elementary Administration Credential; Principal, Muscoy Elementary School, San Bernardino City Unified School District, California.

Elinor R. Stallard, B.A., M.A. in Counseling, Life Credential California Elementary Schools; Pupil Personnel Services with School Psychologists Authorization, Montclair School District, Ontario, California.

Thomas B. Stallard, A.B., M.S., General Secondary Certification in Kansas, Life Certification in California, Mathematics Instructor, Chaffey High School, Ontario, California.

Marjorie R. Wheeler, A.B., Third and Fourth Grade Teacher in California School, San Bernardino City Unified School District, San Bernardino, California.

Contents

        LITTLE HYPOCHONDRIACS (Continued)

        The Characteristics of the "Special Case" 103
        Determining to What Extent a Child Is Becoming a
            "Special Case" 104
        Guidelines in Determining Whether a "Special Case"
            Is Developing 105
        How to Handle the Child Who Has Become a "Special Case" 106
        Guidelines as You Counsel the Child Who Has Become a
            "Special Case" 106

12. FANTASYLAND: WORLD OF ESCAPE FOR
        LITTLE DAYDREAMERS 108

        Guidelines to Control Daydreaming Patterns in the
            Normal Child 109
        Evaluating the Courses of Action 112
        The Characteristics of the "Special Case" 112
        Determining to What Extent a Child Is Becoming a
            "Special Case" 114
        How to Handle the Child Who Has Become a "Special Case" 115
        Guidelines as You Counsel The Child Who Has Become a
            "Special Case" 116

13. LITTLE THUMBSUCKERS AND
        NAILBITERS NEED LOVE 118

        Guidelines to Control Thumbsucking and Nailbiting in
            the Normal Child 120
        Evaluating the Courses of Action 122
        The Characteristics of the "Special Case" 123
        Guidelines for Pinpointing the Characteristics of the
            "Special Case" 124
        Determining to What Extent a Child Is Becoming a
            "Special Case" 124
        How to Handle the Child Who Has Become a "Special Case" 125

14. FIRE-PLAYERS AND LITTLE FIRE-SETTERS 128

        Guidelines to Control Fire-Setting in the Normal Child 129
        Evaluating the Courses of Action 131
        The Characteristics of the "Special Case" 131
        Guidelines for Pinpointing the Characteristics of the
            "Special Case" 133
        Determining to What Extent a Child Is Becoming a
            "Special Case" 134

1

Teachers Are
Human Beings Too

The wise and mature counselor accepts his capabilities as well as his limitations.

As you digest the chapters of this book, apply the guidelines and sample checklists (in the Appendix) to the realities of your classroom.

How can you utilize them to help you and your students? In the complex picture of helping the normal child who has become a "special case," you will become increasingly aware that the most important catalyst is you, the teacher. The counseling techniques and supportive material you use must fit your personality and your concept of your role as a teacher. You are the one who will probably:

- First spot the emerging "special case."
- Decide what may or may not be done.
- In most instances, carry out any program of counseling.
- Be the first to inform your administration and school specialists.
- Handle the delicate problem of counseling the parents.
- Make a referral for outside psychological or medical help.

Many continuous and ever-increasing demands fall upon you, the teacher. Therefore, when it comes to counseling your "special case," it is imperative that you become as aware as possible of your own abilities, capacities, and limitations. As the use of teacher aids and other types of classroom-support personnel grows in our school systems, the teacher will be relieved of more and more tedious, administrative tasks. She will be given more time for testing, counseling, and evaluating.

Slowly your teaching experience broadens. Your capabilities in coping with your students and their problems increase. Each year should find you more productive and more astute in counseling your "special cases." With this growth, however, goes caution—know your limitations. You are not a psychologist, a social worker, or a physician—do not attempt to be one. Ask for help, assistance, or guidance when you need it. Refer your "special case" promptly, before you lose control. Fear too frequently may force you to postpone making a needed decision. Immediately, as it emerges, share the burden of your "special case" with your administration and school specialists.

SYMPATHY vs. EMPATHY

As an individual, a human being, and a teacher, you are fully aware of how difficult it is to remain emotionally uninvolved with your students. They are lovable. They do things that make you angry. They need you and show this need. Easily you see your own hopes, desires, and problems in your students. Yet, to be truly effective, the good teacher maintains an emotional detachment from the problems of her students. She attempts to understand these problems, accepts the child as he is, and establishes a climate that can enable him to grow and mature physically, mentally, emotionally, and socially.

There is a vast difference between sympathy and empathy. The sympathetic teacher identifies with the child, suffers with him, and is emotionally involved in his successes and failures. The teacher who expresses empathy understands him and accepts him with warmth and love. Successful counseling requires empathy.

THERE SHOULD BE A PRICE TO PAY

From an individualistic point of view, greater success is usually attained in counseling if you, the counselor, are able to project to the patient or client the feeling, "this will cost me something." Money may or may not be part of that "something," but the cost most certainly will involve effort, time, loss of certain goals to attain others, energy expended, and work. This concept of personal cost is important to the success and to the effort expended in any counseling situation. As you counsel, it is a factor that needs to be stressed with your "special case," as well as with his parents.

HONESTY PAYS DIVIDENDS

Be honest with yourself and others, your "special case," his parents, administrators, specialists, and referrals when you:

- Explain the problem.
- Outline what you have done.
- Define your limits in counseling this "special case."
- Indicate what courses of action you feel may have to be followed and what results may be expected.
- Give specific do's and don'ts for the parents as they try to improve their interpersonal relations in helping your "special case," their son or daughter, return to more normal behavior patterns.
- Counsel your "special case" concerning the extent and potentials of his behavior problems.

Too frequently, a teacher feels that if she is too honest, those involved, such as administrators, parents, and child, may be hurt. This is not true. What is important is how you communicate. People want to know the truth. Even the most unfavorable situation or development, if stated with compassion and understanding, is more acceptable than half truths or silence. Most people appreciate a sincere, straightforward answer, even if it's "I don't know."

Stress to the parent, or to the parent-substitute, how important it is that he personally "carry the ball," so to speak. Each "special case" needs to know that his parent, or someone in the parent role, cares. Developing interests in his child, whether the parent really has such interests or not, is essential if he is going to help and support you in your counseling efforts. True, your counseling can be effective without parental support, but it is more difficult.

Each parent needs to know that if the problems of the "special case" increase and the child's ability to cope with his environment deteriorates, the emotional and physical expenses to all concerned will rise. Financial expenditure will be incurred if the child must be referred for psychological and/or medical help, or if the community juvenile authorities eventually step in and require legal responsibility of the parents.

Unless both parents and the child feel in some way that the help they are receiving from you involves an investment on their part, in effort, time, or money:

- Your job becomes much more difficult.
- Your chances of success decrease.
- Your own personal frustrations increase.

Counseling your "special case" is always difficult. For success, you need everything in your favor, in every way possible:

- Your own self confidence.
- The confidence of others.
- Knowledge of the problem.
- Techniques to use in counseling.
- Awareness of what limitations your administration and school district place on you in the counseling role.
- What can and cannot be accomplished.

Above all, recognize that you are a human being with many capabilities, various capacities, and specific limitations. Accept yourself as you are.

SOME SUCCESSFUL TECHNIQUES IN COUNSELING

Experience is the most effective teacher. As you experiment, you develop techniques that fit your personality. These then become effective for you, not only in your counseling of students, but also in your relationships with parents, other teachers, and administrators.

You probably use two types of counseling—non-directive and directive. In non-directive counseling, you tend to let the child take the initiative. You may reflect his feelings; that is, you listen to what he says, repeat the thought or idea back to him, either in the same set of words or in a different set. As an example, a child might say, "I don't like the principal." You could return the idea to him as, "Oh, you mean you dislike him at times." You may then let him talk on, or sum up what you feel he has said and ask his reaction. Other indirect techniques involve allowing a group (group therapy) to talk about a particular behavior or school problem its members are having. Another indirect technique might be to structure a game or classroom situation to demonstrate a particular difficulty. In this learning situation, the children apparently stumble upon the problem or possible solutions themselves.

Direct counseling may be involved as you discuss an area of anxiety with a child and point out (subtly or otherwise) possible solutions, the consequences of these solutions, his responsibilities, etc. The amount of permissiveness, the limitations you place in the counseling situation, your approving, disapproving, or merely accepting attitudes, all become part of your techniques to structure or manipulate a counseling situation.

You will be surprised at how much counseling you can do with a child if you will actually sit on the floor with him and talk as you play with puzzles, building blocks, etc. Listen; seek his opinion. How does he feel—physically, mentally, emotionally, and socially? Ask him; he usually will tell you. This type of supportive therapy, performed either directively or non-directively, or as a combination of both, gets results.

GUIDELINES FOR DEFINING YOUR COUNSELING ROLE

Keep a record, mental if not written, of possible limits of your physical capacity. How many hours a day each week are you capable of working before your effectiveness begins to deteriorate? At what times of the day, week, or month, do you physically function best? If you are a woman, is there a relation between your menstrual cycle and your effectiveness? When during the year (for example, around Christmas, or at school term beginning or ending) are you especially tired or do you tend to function at a lower level?

Like physical limitations, know the limitations of your mental and emotional capacities. When do you function best—morning, evening, beginnings or endings of the week? In what ways are these functions limited or controlled? How are they related to events at home or at school? For example: What happens to your ability to counsel when your own sickness or that of others in your family is involved? In what way is your ability to perform curtailed by such items as job insecurity, financial stresses, and other economic, social, and religious problems?

Outside controls are also placed on your role as a counselor. Every school, every school district, and every community is different. You must limit the amount, the technique, and the extent of your counseling to what is acceptable in a teacher-pupil relationship, appropriate to the societies in which you live. Most school administrations are quite specific about teacher counseling and what is and is not allowed. Know what their guidelines are, and adhere to them.

Likewise, there are legal limitations as to what you may and may not do. You certainly cannot practice medicine or clinical psychology. In many states, there are very specific laws defining the counseling of teachers, administrators, and even school psychologists. These are often spelled out in legislation. Be aware of the legal limitations and conform your counseling well within the possible interpretations of such limits.

Be assured that the warmth, understanding, support, and interpretation you give through counseling will have a greater effect on your students than you will probably ever realize. Granted, there always will be a few you will fail to help in any way. Accept this as par for the course. However, individuals express appreciation in many ways. Some may be aware of your help, but they may be unable to thank you. Some may only realize, years later, how important you were to their growth and development. And others may never realize it.

Each of us wants to be appreciated When administrators, parents, and children recognize and express their gratitude for what we have done in counseling, this is part of our reward. Another part, and perhaps the greatest, is the inner feeling of warmth and accomplishment sensed when we know we have helped a child find a firm path in his or her desire to mature and succeed.

2

When Do You
Holler For Help?

*It's a sign of strength in a teacher
to know when to seek assistance.*

Each of us has problems. When do we try to resolve them ourselves and when do we "holler for help"? It's best to holler for
help *before* the water is too deep!

Where does your help come from? That depends upon the problem, its immediacy, its extent, and how well equipped you are to
handle the help you get. Help may come from an associate, from
past experience, from a book, or from an authority more qualified
to solve the particular problem than yourself.

However, the best help often comes from within yourself. It is
a compilation and application of the principles that you have gained
from many sources. This book is such a source. Its guidelines and
checklists can help you as you counsel your normal elementary
school child. Furthermore, they can assist you in deciding when
to seek help.

As you read and personally apply the principles and techniques
in this book it is important to know that they can be effective in
some 99 out of a 100 of your "special case" situations. In every
classroom, the potential of a "special case" is always present. A
"special case" materializes when the normal irritants or behavior
characteristics of any child become unacceptable. This unacceptability may be a result of failure of discipline, failure of control, or
breakdown in any phase of the child's day-to-day living. These
"special case" problems are resolvable.

You, the elementary school teacher, have a responsibility to help every student adjust to the school way of life. Some students accomplish this adjustment easily and readily. Others, due to emotional, mental, and physical factors, encounter difficulty. Then they may become problem children in your classroom, at least until a readjustment occurs. Any readjustment, however, must be reinforced sufficiently to be established as the child's normal behavior pattern.

This book presents positive guidelines to help you aid your little problem "psyches" to make this adjustment. Like each of us, every child has a "psyche" of his own.

"PSYCHE" MEANS "SPIRIT, LIFE, SOUL, OR MIND"

Modern psychiatry regards the "psyche" as an organ of the individual. It is treated as such here. Like any of our other organs, including the cerebral and the endocrinal, it has its own functions. It reaches all parts of the body and it serves to adjust the entire individual to his personal needs, and the demands of his environment.

Just as the cerebral or endocrinal system may fail to function and may require medical treatment, so the psychic system may fail and need psychological help.

As the well-known saying goes, "An ounce of prevention is worth a pound of cure," and when it comes to emotional problems, it's worth several pounds, especially with children. Therefore, as a teacher being unemotionally involved, you are in a key position to provide such preventive support.

HELP EACH STUDENT ADJUST

The guidelines, techniques, and checklists in this book provide positive approaches. They can help you recognize emerging difficulties in the psychic system and pinpoint the child or children who merely need to adjust, those who are becoming "special cases," or those who need possibly to be referred to a school specialist. In addition, they can guide you as you cope with each case and resolve each problem in the best interests of the child, school, and the community. The guidelines and checklists concern problems which are specifically "psyche" oriented. They are just as effective with the average student as with the "special case." Every child needs to be listened to. He needs to feel important, be accepted, show off his specific abilities, and be a leader as well as a follower. As you help each child recognize and accept his role, his limitations, and his capacities, you are counseling and helping him adjust to the school of life.

These guidelines and techniques can assist you in the administering of rewards and punishments. They help you control and guide your students in the learning situation, at play, and in the school environment. You acquire them from instructors, practice teaching, and from your personal observation and experience. They may be as simple as raising or lowering your voice to control the class using colored stars for achievement, or placing a child in a certain seat to stimulate thinking.

Keeping detailed chronological reports on every student or even on just the "special cases," is oftentimes unrealistic and impractical for the average classroom teacher. This is certainly true if you have four or five "special cases" in your classroom. However, the amount of details and how they are recorded, is very flexible. In any case, some notes on the most critical situations are essential. The way in which you keep such records will evolve as your experience grows The beginning teacher may find the keeping of even minimal notes on a child's behavior almost impossible because of other administrative and teaching demands. No one does everything at once, but if you can realistically be aware of the goals you hope to attain, you will slowly improve your efficiency and capacity to help each child grow. It is most important for any beginning teacher, or for that matter, any teacher who is try'ng to develop an entirely different approach to her profession, to accept the following axioms:

- Any change is a slow process. We evolve from one pattern to the next. Accept your often painful process of growth.
- As you counsel, establish both short-term and long-term goals in terms of the results you desire. This is true for yourself as well as for your students.
- Do not hesitate to "holler for help." Usually, help is readily available, but personal fear and a hesitancy to annoy others often keeps us from asking.

THE "SPECIAL CASE"

The normal child, by definition, is a physically, emotionally, and mentally healthy individual who adjusts easily to the classroom and playground environment around him. He tends to be cooperative, enters into the daily routine, and—by and large—accepts and is accepted by his superiors, inferiors, and peers.

Any normal child may become a "special case" when a serious physical, emotional, or mental imbalance occurs. This imbalance may be caused by internal or external stresses and pressures. Internal pressures may be generated by his own fears or fancies, as well as from organic anomalies. External pressures may originate within the community, at home, at school, or at play.

Although any individual cause, or combination of causes, might conceivably project the normal child into the status of a "special case," once the causes of the imbalance are resolved, the "special case" should return to normal. If return to normal does not occur, the individual may be regarded, at least potentially, as a "special case" in need of referral to a school specialist.

The "special case" in this book is *not* defined as an acute neurotic or a psychotic personality. He is merely a child who is in need of additional educational, disciplinary and psychological help by you, your principal, or members of your Pupil Personnel staff. Granted, in a certain percentage of incidents, he may develop into a "special case" who needs professional psychological counsel and will need to be referred. In the main, the material in these chapters can help you in your positive relationship with the normal child who has, for a time, become a "special case."

It is not the responsibility of a classroom teacher to decide whether or not a child is normal. However, the teacher is usually the first to become aware of a potentially serious problem and report it. Your opinion and evaluation will be sought. There are many ways in which you can be prepared to help the specialist involved. The most effective help you can furnish will be in maintaining an accurate chronological report of the "special case." The guidelines and checklists presented in this book should form the basis for your record.

Fortunately, very few "special cases" need referral. Problems of the "psyche," like the mumps and measles, are always with us.

EACH CRISIS CAN HELP US MATURE

Every child suffers from innumerable personal catastrophes. These may be as traumatic as death in the family, possible family break-up or divorce, serious illness, acute fears, or accidents involving major bodily harm. On the other hand, they may be as normal as problems of maturation, outbursts of aggression, simple lacerations, or any one of the many stresses forced upon a child by the complexities of a demanding society. With each catastrophe, there comes a crisis. If it is well met, a beneficial part of the growing-up process has been achieved. On the other hand, several unsatisfactorily met crises can put the normal child into the temporary classification of the "special case."

The alert teacher spots the crisis and provides effective support in helping the child. This support may come from: (a) the teacher's general "bag of tricks," (b) the guidance of administration and consulting specialists, and (c) the specifically oriented guidelines given in this book.

The following chapters offer you, the teacher, as well as the teacher-administrator team, specifics relating to behavior problems, emotional disturbances, and social maladjustment patterns that are symptomatic of the "special case." These involve excessive attention, withdrawing, excessive body movements, oversensitivity, enjoyed illness, daydreaming, nailbiting and thumbsucking, hostility, cruelty, stealing, lying, cheating, firesetting, refusing to conform, and resisting discipline.

3

The Administration
Answers Your SOS

*The chain of command is your life
line.*

"Doctor Miller, I'm in hot water!" The voice was that of a young
girl, desperately sending an SOS out over the telephone. "I can't
discuss my problem over the phone. Can I see you immediately?"

Given an appointment, Miss Mary L. arrived later in the day,
still extremely agitated. She was attractive, rather petite, well
groomed, and soft-spoken. This was her first year as an elementary
school teacher. Her dilemma centered around two children whose
excessive hostility threatened her control of the classroom.

"And Dr. Miller, I can't get it back. They're bullying me. What's
the matter with me? I never had this trouble in my practice teaching! What can I do?"

"What does your principal say?"

"He hasn't said anything. Every time he visits my class they're
all as good as gold, and I'm afraid to tell him how bad they are.
Either he won't believe me, or it may be a mark against me, and
then I face not being rehired."

Mary L. had acted well. She recognized that she had a problem,
and she sought help. However, her fear was so great that she failed
to use her most effective resources. As we talked, she struggled with
the problem.

12

"How would my strength as a teacher best be advanced through the judicious use of the school's chain of command system?

"I just don't see why I have to tell him," she protested.

"For several reasons, Mary. First, sooner or later, any problem that continues to grow in the school environment is going to come to the attention of the administration. Second, it will most likely come at a time when you are least prepared to handle it. Third, it may come in a way that could really jeopardize your future. And fourth, it might even come at a time when your principal is overloaded and in no mood to handle it.

"By communicating with your principal as the problem is developing, you will receive his guidance, and his support. At the same time, you will alert him to the possibility that your problem may even develop into a school problem."

While Miss L. did not interrupt, her look was both questioning and concerned.

"I'm awfully glad, Mary, that you faced this situation immediately instead of letting it ride. Loyalty and confidence, up and down, are keys to any successful teacher-administrator team."

Mary L. found these keys as soon as she took her problem to her principal. He supported her, and he showed her little techniques in discipline and psychological motivation that resolved this particular situation.

Her principal provided that answer to her SOS. The chain of command was her lifeline. The action she was afraid to take, because she felt it would jeopardize her future, became the foundation for the establishment of a strong and positive teacher-administrator relationship. In addition, her action became a lifeline to the two "bullying" pupils, and they did not become "special cases."

YOUR SCHOOL IS STUDENT ORIENTED

Although most school children are not generally too aware of the fact, they are "top man" in the educational system. Next to the students comes you, the classroom teacher. In the main, all the administration, the specialists, the supportive personnel, the physical plant, and the equipment of a school system serve only one purpose: That purpose is to help you, the teacher, achieve your primary mission, to educate and prepare the child in becoming a responsible member of his society.

A school's sole reason for existence is its students. All of the expenditures of money, equipment, time, and human effort are worthwhile when this mission is accomplished.

The school is pupil-centered. In the same vein, the school then becomes the child's second home. Whether male or female, the teacher tends to assume the mother role. The administrator becomes the father figure as far as the child is concerned.

Therefore, the more cooperative and harmonious the relationship between you and your administrator, the more secure your students will feel, and the greater your success will be in teaching and counseling the child who becomes or who may become a "special case."

As was discussed with Miss Mary L., the principal, like the father in a family group, is always in a much better position to cope with the problems of his growing children if his wife treats him with respect and keeps him continuously informed. This is not only true with problems that are in existence, but with potential problems that may be developing.

On the other hand, the relationship in the good administrative-teacher team requires that the mother figure be respected and never put in a position of ridicule or public blame.

In the home situation, it may be advisable that the children participate in differences of opinion that involve them. They then become aware that their parents do not always agree. However, the school climate is usually much better if differences of opinion among the faculty and administration are resolved behind closed doors at the proper time and place.

To the child, the higher echelons in the school's administrative system are pretty much in the realm of the divine. He knows that such superiors exist, but he is relatively unaware of how they function and of their responsibilities. He is able to sense, and often act, on the fear, dislike, and respect that these individuals arouse in you.

Normally, a child is oriented to those around him who curtail as well as fulfill his needs. Therefore, you, the wise teacher, will provide opportunities for each student to assume various roles under your supervision, even in the most elementary class.

Give him "leadership" and "fellowship." Thus, he will be conditioned to accept one of the greatest realities of life.

WHEN ALL IS NOT SMOOTH

In this day of active, as well as passive, teacher grievance and teacher militancy, not all teachers receive satisfaction or the interpersonal relationships they seek from discussions with their principals, other supervisors, or even from support and special services personnel. When this appears to be the case, attempt to determine the real source of the impasse. Is it yourself? Is it the situation and environment? Is it the temperament and characteristics of those who are supposed to help you? Or is it a personality conflict?

How you cope with the problem and whether you keep the relations and communications as effective as possible depends upon your capacities. You may find the only solution you can work with is a civil truce where you protect yourself, but do not antagonize the situation by seeking confrontation or undermining supervision personnel. Since such a solution is never really rewarding, it may be best after weighing all factors to find another and more satisfying school situation. If you appear to be in the minority, perhaps the difficulty is with you. If others live with and grow in the situation you feel uninspired in, perhaps you as a teacher have not been able to develop cooperative interpersonal relationships with administrators and supervisors.

How you develop your own ethical attitudes and professional loyalties is important. Each of us needs to be cooperatively involved in school policy and philosophy. We need continual intellectual improvement, the development of positive and productive ethical attitudes, and the increasing professional loyalty to ourselves as well as to those around us. This is never easy, but it can be done.

There are many professional and trade publications on the art of getting along with, learning to live with, and influencing peers, as well as superiors and those who work for you. Attempt to apply the principles they suggest. From observation and by simple questioning, find out how the teacher or teachers you admire most are accomplishing the goals you desire. At times, even presenting the problem lucidly to the administration in a one-to-one conference is extremely effective. When several individuals are involved, the formation of a faculty committee to look into and seek solutions to grievances and problems between the administration, faculty, and support personnel, may be the realistic approach. This is frequently the key where a power struggle has developed and individual members of the staff have found it impossible to communicate adequately.

THERE'S A "CHAIN OF COMMAND" IN EVERYTHING

The sooner the child recognizes the various links in the many chains of command that he is involved with, the more sophisticated he becomes in his relationships. The more knowledgable or sophisticated he becomes, the smoother his interpersonal relations become. He learns more quickly; he functions better; and he lives a more adjusted life.

First and foremost in the chains of command, he must live with those at home. His home is the world and center of his preschool life. However, in kindergarten he faces new chains of command, perhaps for the first time in his life. Therefore, it is imperative that he be given a consistent example of accepting, and participating in, the school's power structure.

ENCOURAGING RESPECT FOR AUTHORITY

1. Support the child's existing chain of command at home, whether or not you can respect it.

Jane A. comes from a broken home that has involved alcoholism of the mother and general child neglect. At present, Jane is in the custody of her father. Even the most casual observer is aware that Jane has found refuge in a withdrawal behavior pattern. She already is a "special case."

In helping Jane, her first grade teacher, Mrs. M. used the child's poor parental background as a basis on which to build a warm, understanding relationship. Mrs. M. talked with Jane about her home and her parents. In no way did Mrs. M. indicate to the child that her parents were to blame, or that the child was different from her classmates because of her home environment.

She understood Jane's love for both parents. With her own consistent support, good communications, and attention, she provided the child with a much-needed strong "good mother" figure. This was not done, however, at the expense of Jane's mother.

2. Support the school's existing chain of command. Your loyalty

unconnected verbalization, and what might be called by many, "strange actions." Often, the child's attention span gets shorter, his ability to concentrate decreases, he may become fearful and tearful for no apparent cause. Logical reasoning tends to break down.

WHEN TO INVOLVE THE PUPIL PERSONNEL STAFF

In educational institutions, and other types as well, discipline has not solved mental health problems. The suggestions and techniques of the authors will help you, the elementary school teacher, in guiding your students to help themselves be effective citizens, and to encourage the education process. This book begins where discipline leaves off. From a practical point, discipline is always a part of every learning situation. It may be imposed by self, by others, or by environment and circumstances. It may be positive or negative. It is essential in any well regulated school, but its value is always limited. The wise teacher combines good disciplinary procedures with the use of the psychological tools and techniques available to her. With human warmth and personal dignity, she attempts to acquire and utilize counseling techniques and supportive therapy. She learns when discipline will work and when it will fail, and that she has at her command many ways of solving problems.

Probably ninety-nine percent of your student's behavior problems, emotional disturbances, and social maladjustments can be resolved using: 1) your classroom control and disciplinary procedures; 2) the techniques presented here under various "special cases"; or 3) a combination of both. However, for the exception, involve your Pupil Personnel staff.

HOW ONE ADMINISTRATION DOES IT

As an example, I asked James Bules, a California elementary school principal, "In your school system, how does a teacher obtain help when she feels she can no longer cope with her 'special case'? How does she actually involve your Pupil Personnel specialists?"

Carefully, he began, "I think you must realize that the problem may conceivably be resolved at any step of the following procedure.

"Let's take, for instance, a child who is emotionally disturbed. He has an adequate I.Q., but is a low achiever, a potential candidate for our 'EH' (Emotionally Handicapped) program.

"First, and this is usually on a very informal basis, the teacher will report the behavior problem or pattern to me. Actually, the teacher's initial report, as well as her request for the involvement of our specialist's programs, depend a great deal on her experience and awareness. She usually senses when a child will or will not fit into the normal classroom environment.

"Much depends on the urgency of the problem. If, for example, the child has just set a fire involving even a minimal amount of damage, the teacher would report the incident immediately. If, on the other hand, this child demonstrated continued outbursts of hostile behavior, the teacher may wait until she has a record that indicates a definite pattern before she brings it to my attention.

"If her initial report requires urgency, I will see the child immediately. If not, I will see him at my earliest convenience. From my point of view, the most important objective at this time is to gain perspective. Some decisions may be postponed. Others must be made without delay. I may: (1) talk with the child; (2) administer punitive measures; (3) return him to or exclude him from class, with all that may entail; (4) involve the parents by telephone; or (5) simply start a written evaluation to be used as a basis for future decisions.

"I make it a point to personally talk with the teacher or teachers involved about the problem. Usually, this occurs after school when interruptions are minimal. I tactfully attempt to assist the teacher with specific classroom and playground procedures to handle this 'special case.'

"Second, when several instances of a definite pattern of unacceptable behavior have come to my attention, and the teacher's as well as my own negative and positive disciplinary measures have failed to produce the desired results, we move to involve others, specifically, the Pupil Personnel team. The teacher initiates the referral and it is processed through my office.

"The teacher puts into writing her evaluation of the problem when she requests referral. Her complete report may be included in the initial request for Pupil Personnel assistance, or it may come later. The latter course is often the case if the teacher wishes to make an extensive and detailed evaluation. Regardless of when the report is done, or even if she makes two reports, the teacher will present her statement of the problem, detailing behavior she feels is pertinent. She will make objective as well as subjective comments, involving the classroom situation, the physical, mental, and emotional adjustments of the child, and any other data that she feels may assist those working on the problem.

"Actually, from this point on, in our system, I as school principal, do not enter into the picture as a decision-maker. The teacher has requested psychological testing or a specialist's evaluation; I forward this request.

"Third, the Pupil Personnel team now becomes involved. The curriculum consultant may very well be the first specialist to consider possible solutions. This is essentially true if the problem student is in the kindergarten or first grade. An evaluation from the curriculum consultant is always obtained if the exclusion of the child from the normal school classroom is contemplated.

"Our school nurse may have seen the child and may have an extensive case history on him. If there is any suspicion of a medical problem, a general physical examination by one of our school physicians will be requested. In this school district, we have a private physician on contract. He examines and reports on any child referred to him through our special services department. Testing depends upon the mental, physical, and/or emotional problems involved. Usually, these will include tests to assess intelligence, emotional maturity, achievement level, perceptual difficulties, and behavioral characteristics. This step and the two that follow would be particularly appropriate in cases involving unacceptable sexual tendencies or behavior.

"Fourth, the school psychologist follows through on the teacher referral and formulates an overall evaluation of the problem, possible solutions, and recommendations for courses of action. The parents may be, and in most cases are, interviewed by the psychologist. Actually, we request written consent from the parents before testing their child. At the same time, we ask for a signed 'authorization for the release of medical and/or psychological information' to us by private individuals, clinics, or agencies that may have seen the child. Granted, we aren't stymied if we don't have these, but it is more realistic if we involve the parents immediately and have their cooperation and written consent.

"Fifth, the guidance department will work directly with the curriculum consultant, the child welfare consultant, and the psychological services department. I think it is important to remember that, at least in our system, the administration does not want any one person to assume the complete responsibility of the disposition of a problem child. Every possible solution is considered and evaluated. No decision is so final that it cannot be modified or changed if the child's welfare can better be served by that change.

"Finally, the recommendations from the school psychologist come back to me, the principal. I contact the parents, have them come in, and personally give them a resume that includes:

- What has happened.
- Where the school stands.
- What can and cannot be done.
- What decisions we have reached.
- What recommendations have been made.
- What may happen in the future.

"As an example, we had the problem of nine year old Tommy M. last year. The M. family had a marriage and family problem. The teacher, Grace B. frankly said, 'I can't cope with the boy.' When I talked with his parents, they said the same thing. We went through the procedure I've just outlined, but our Pupil Personnel team decided that Tommy was not eligible for our 'EH' program. This decision was reached because of faculty limitation. Tommy went back to the classroom. I worked with Miss B. and we incorporated suggestions from our consulting specialists. The interpersonal relationship of the entire class improved. We were able to help Tommy adjust to Miss B.'s classroom program. Tommy's family cooperated and Tommy and both parents saw a private family counselor. The family problems decreased and so far this year, we have had no problems with Tommy that we were unable to solve adequately.

"After kindergarten and the first grade, we just won't exclude students from our school situation until every possibility is exhausted. We really hit rock bottom before we 'throw in the sponge,' so to speak. Even before we inaugurated our 'EH' program, we would put a youngster on a partial day schedule rather than eliminate him."

It is probably true that expulsion for a short term should be used more often; however, in most areas some form of federal and/or state subsidization based on "average daily attendance" puts pressure on an administration to consider other factors and not solely the welfare of the child.

Principal James Bules' description of how a teacher in his school system utilizes the services of the Pupil Personnel departments is fairly typical. I think it is important to note that even though procedures vary from district to district, these specialists are there to help.

SERVICES PUPIL PERSONNEL SPECIALISTS OFFER

Your Pupil Personnel team is constantly trying to provide you with information, techniques, and knowledge. These specialists are not a part of your school system just to take a problem case off your hands and put him somewhere else. You must take advantage of their program. They will offer it to you, but will not force you to participate. Their in-service meetings, personal interviews, staff meetings, lectures, and workshops are available to help you better understand your pupils and yourself, but you must take the time to attend them. Ask your administrator, "What is available?" "Where do I go to take part in such training programs?" "When do they occur?" Your contacts with your Pupil Personnel team will enable you to: (1) improve yourself and your teaching capacities; and (2) guide and support you in your efforts as you help your "special case" adjust to his school environment.

The question always arises, "Well, just what does a school psychologist do?" or for that matter, "What does each member of the Pupil Personnel team do?" This question may be answered personally or from the material distributed by your own Special Services department. Each department lists what is available, how it is obtained, and in what ways you may profit by its services.

As an example, the psychologist may only supervise psychometrists who actually do the testing, evaluating, and presenting of recommendations. He may devote much of his time to public relations, inservice training programs, and specific thorny problems involving the clinical psychological techniques of the staff and the relationships that involve other departments and other disciplines. He may actually be involved in clinical psychological therapy programs, working with children as well as with their families.

His job will vary depending upon: (a) the particular elementary school system; (b) the availability of other specialists; (c) the acceptance of his profession by teachers, administrators and the community; and (d) what is specifically requested by the administration and school board that employ him.

For example, facilities may be as limited as that of a small, mid-western consolidated school district, whose funds allow the part-time employment of a psychologist. Her primary function really is that of education. In the several scattered communities that make up her school district, she continuously speaks before various P.T.A., church, and civic groups. She schedules special teacher's meetings at the schools and starts in-service training programs designed to acquaint administration and teachers alike with what can be done with the available resources and what they can strive for as future goals. She initiates limited testing programs. She discovers that one of the system's teachers had some speech therapy training. This teacher agrees to hold a special session after school once a week for a limited number of speech-handicapped children. Her program starts successfully and slowly grows.

Almost at the other end of the spectrum, a relatively large western school district offers almost a complete range of Pupil Personnel services. They provide in-service training programs, lecture series, and special programs for administration and teachers. Testing is available as needed. According to need, members of the team attend post-graduate classes on a regular basis. There are specialists in nearly all areas, including personnel to conduct research into the effectiveness of various approaches to different problems. A play therapy program is available at a central location that is properly staffed and equipped for a specific number of emotionally handi-capped children. This program is on a one-to-one, one teacher-therapist to one pupil, basis. This is an extremely expensive opera-tion, but one that will probably come to many districts in the future for no other reason than it is a logical extension of the special programs a school system might be expected to provide.

USE ALL YOUR RESOURCES

The ideas, guidelines, and specific techniques in this book should be combined with your normally improving disciplinary techniques and your customary teaching skills. They will be most useful as you work with the "special case" who will not be removed from your classroom and for whom you have the responsibility of helping to ad-just to a normal school environment. Use every resource available to you: your own skill as a teacher, the suggestions here, and the information the psychologist or other members in your Pupil Personnel staff make available to you.

Too frequently, you the teacher are not prepared to carry out a specialist's recommendations, particularly if the specialist comes in, makes his recommendation, and leaves. If there are no specialists, you are even less prepared. This book can fill this gap and it can be your own personal specialist.

GUIDELINES FOR UTILIZING SPECIALISTS

1. Personally acquaint yourself with each available member of your Pupil Personnel team. Talk with your administrator and other teachers about the *what, when, where,* and *how* of each of the services available to you. Do this at the beginning of every year. In this way you re-acquaint yourself with the services at hand. You also become informed about what is new.

2. Seek out and participate in special lectures, workships, demonstrations, and in-service training programs sponsored by your special services departments. Here you will learn specific techniques, new information about what is available, and what may be available in the future as far as your school system is concerned.

3. Consistently re-evaluate your own program, your procedures for resolving "special cases," your personal relationships with your administration, and your specialists. Are you profiting from everything that is available to you? How could it be improved upon?

5

Parents and Siblings
Complicate the Picture

Observe the behavior pattern of the parent, and you will gain insight into how to counsel your "special case."

When it comes to counseling the "special case," you the teacher must never lose sight of the fact that the child is the product of his home. Parents and siblings are human beings. They are variable, changeable, unpredictable, inconsistent, and very definitely primary shapers and movers in the changing personality of your "special case."

Jack P. taught his first year in a low income district. Confidently, he prepared for his first fall session of parent-teacher conferences. Frustrated and somewhat despondent at the end of the second day of scheduled conferences, he went to his principal. "I failed you; what in the world did I do wrong?"

"How do you mean you failed me?"

"I sent out my parent-teacher conference notices. The majority were returned; but so far only three parents have shown up out of twelve scheduled to come. I don't know what to do."

"Jack, that's a better average than we usually have. It's twenty-five percent, and for this school you've done really well. We just don't have many parents who are willing or able to cooperate. This is why I encourage teachers to visit the homes of their students if possible. Don't forget, these parents have feelings too. They're afraid, not just of authority or of the school in general, but of anything

28

that might make them conform to a society they don't feel a part of."

Jack's principal was right. People react in the manner that is normal to their environment.

HOW TO DEAL WITH PARENTS AND SIBLINGS OF THE "SPECIAL CASE"

The majority of parents with whom you come in contact, regardless of whether their child has become a "special case" or not, will be female. Fathers of elementary school children tend to delegate to their wives the responsibility of the children. This includes coping with school problems. Even where a father's interest is high, work commitments often keep him from parent-teacher conferences scheduled during his work day.

To really encourage the father of a child who is a "special case," to attend your parent-teacher conferences, schedule a late afternoon or evening appointment. Home visits, back-to-school nights, school carnivals, and evening P.T.A. meetings are positive ways to enlist the interest and cooperation of a father.

Mothers of elementary school children, like many of us, often feel trapped or caught in the middle. They are bombarded by innumerable chores and crises. They respond to the most urgent demand. For instance, a mother who has a parent conference at 3:30 P.M. may have to take care of her two-year-old with a cut hand at 3:00 P.M. She may arrive late, or not at all.

Consider the order of siblings in the family. Your parent relationships will be affected by this order. There is no "pigeon-hole" into which you can slide each case. The oldest sibling has a different home environment from the middle child or from the youngest, even though they come from the same home. Family conditions vary from year to year through the growing years, and each child responds differently.

Your relationships with parents, particularly the mother, will be less frustrating and more rewarding if you allow for inconsistencies and omissions, and at the same time maintain your own planned schedule. Do the best you can with the time, the facilities, and the cooperation that is given you.

The behavior patterns of a woman with several young children will, in the average, tend to be more unpredictable and less consistent than those of the woman who has no family, or whose children are in the later school years and who is following a regulated daily schedule. The is true simply because unforeseen emergencies occur when young children are in the home.

Almost every parent is basically hostile to any authority figure in an official or semi-official capacity whose communications, verbal or written, can be interpreted as an invasion of family privacy. Just the idea of a note from school, or the possibility of having to account for his child's unacceptable acts is a threat.

IDENTIFYING WITH YOUR PUPIL'S BACKGROUND

Each teacher must discover for himself the sociological structure of the community from which his students come. Accept the fact that physical neglect relating to food, shelter, and clothing exists in every strata of life. Even in homes where every physical need is met, the neglect of emotional needs may still be devastating to the security of the parents and of the children.

Your observations will indicate that parental physical and verbal brutality toward children is more common than statistics would lead us to believe. The excessive use of alcohol, as well as drugs, creates instability in many homes. The incidence of female alcoholism appears to be increasing. It is often difficult to detect because families protect and shelter the alcholic wife and mother.

Be aware that physical or emotional ill health in the family, and especially over an extended period, may cause problems of child neglect, or provide a fertile field for family conflicts. And unfortunately, broken homes are part of the American way of life. In some areas, the divorce rate is almost as high as the marriage rate.

Maralyn F., a fourth grade teacher for a unified school district. vividly pinpointed some of the potential difficulty. She quoted the mother of a student who had children by her previous as well as her present marriage, and whose husband had children by a previous marriage. "Around our house it's your kids, my kids, and our kids. Fortunately, we all get along."

It's difficult to cope with your pupil's home environment. In counseling the "special case," it is well to remember:

- Twenty-five percent of our marriages end in divorce.
- Our population is a mobile one. It is not uncommon to find a family that has moved an average of ten times in ten years.

- Countless undetermined numbers of family separations frequently occur due to employment, military needs, financial, and family problems. These always involve shifting situations for a child. In addition, and especially in the relatively higher and lower economic levels, arrangements as to who is responsible for the child often fluctuate.
- In establishing your parent-teacher relationships, you may find that you are dealing with the two natural parents, a single natural parent, a foster parent, a relative, or a family friend in the parent role, a step-parent situation, a guardian, or an official (of a public or private agency) having custody of the child.

SUPPORT THE PARENTS—YOU CAN'T CHANGE THEIR HOME

You may discover, or have reason to suspect, that the behavior patterns in the household adversely affect your "special case" student. Whether the circumstances are abnormal or merely inadequate, for all practical purposes, you are powerless to change the child's home environment.

Therefore, you the teacher must work with a current situation as it exists, and with the parents as they are—human beings trying to survive in the environment in which they find themselves.

GUIDELINES FOR SUPPORTING THE FAMILY

1. Accept the child's home life as it is. Except in instances where your suggestions are asked for by receptive parents, you will have little influence upon a specific home. Use the child's home life as the base on which you build your relationship with him.

2. *Empathize* with the child's feelings—don't *sympathize* with him. Refrain from becoming emotionally involved in his problems.

3. In one way or other, each child must learn to live with and to interrelate with his siblings. Support him and let him talk about his brothers and sisters. As he talks, he will personally evaluate ways to better cope with siblings.

4. You see parents in only one or two sets of situations. Be "leery" about jumping to conclusions or giving too much weight to the

evidence gleaned from a child's casual remark, especially when you appear to be a sympathetic listener. More than one teacher has become uncomfortably involved because a student's imagination —stimulated by television, films, etc.—has concocted a likely tale.

5. It is not your privilege, nor duty, to intercede for the child against one parent or both.

6. If you suspect illegal activities on the part of the parents, or even the child, report your suspicions to your administrator. He will inform the proper authorities.

7. For your own protection, and for that of your school system, make complete notations in your classroom records. Use the check-lists, such as are given in the appendix, to discover, to evaluate, and to report to your administration the situations where the home life appears to be a critical factor in the "special case" behavior pattern.

The "special case," like any child, is the product of his home. Since children are imitators, their behavior patterns may well give you strong indications of parental behavior.

UTILIZING PARENTS AND SIBLINGS

The parents, or the parent substitutes and siblings of your "special case," as is true of all your students, will fall into three categories: (1) those who are willing to help; (2) those who can't or don't care; and (3) those who refuse to help.

Typical of the first, those who are willing to help, was Mrs. Helen W., mother of nine-year-old Joan. She never missed a parent-teacher conference; she attended P.T.A. meetings periodically, and was active in the elementary school parent-child programs. She wanted to, and was able to, help, at least up until Joan entered fourth grade.

Joan's behavior changed noticeably. She became a "special case." She was moody and withdrew from the group. Overt hostile acts began to occur. Anticipating the usual parent cooperation, her fourth grade teacher, Miss V., requested a special parent-teacher conference. Mrs. W. signed the request slip, but never appeared for the conference. The subsequent chain of events involved Joan in a playground altercation in which her front tooth was broken. The following morning Mrs. W. arrived at the administrator's office. A perceptive principal soon uncovered the basic circumstances which had made Joan a "special case" in such a short time.

Joan's father, a used car salesman, had left home in August. Since then, there had been little income. To make the house and car payments, and provide food for herself and her two children, Mrs. W. had gone to work as a waitress. Insecure, frantic at her losses, and vainly attempting to maintain her shattered pride, Mrs. W. had all she could do to provide the bare essentials for existence. At this point, she was in no position financially, physically, or emotionally, to give her children the support they so desperately needed. Joan and her little sister had been left more and more to shift for themselves. The results were disastrous.

Almost hysterically, Mrs. W. told the principal, "I'm willing to do anything to help my children. I can see what's happening to Joan. She was so sweet, and now she's moody and seems to be constantly fighting. But I'm just exhausted, and I don't know where to turn or what to do."

There are many parents in this first category, who are able to help their "special case" children. Some, just as Mrs. W., are willing to help, but they, through special circumstances, have changed from the first to the second category. Either temporarily or permanently, they are just incapable of providing adequate parental assistance and understanding for their child.

Of those parents who are both willing and able to help, many just plain do not know what to do. A "special case" child may often be returned to his norm if a willing parent has a few specific suggestions to follow. This parent, where his child is concerned, is usually most amenable to suggestions for a medical examination, if you suspect a physical anomaly; a psychological examination, if necessary; additional tutoring, or possible other professional referral. With your recommendations, a willing parent will often be able to augment the school's curriculum, and to provide at home the additional enriching programs.

For the parent who refuses to help, there remains your capacity to work with the child. Often when a parent is unwilling, there are older siblings who can and will cooperate with you. You may be able to provide them with guidance and specific plans as they interact with their brother or sister whom you feel is becoming the "special case."

GUIDELINES FOR THE PARENT-TEACHER CONFERENCE

1 It is extremely important that the parent-teacher conference be planned and structured to attain the utmost benefit for all concerned. This planning should involve a thorough use of your checklists. It must be in line with your administration's format on such conferences. If you write down, step-by-step, what you propose to discuss and what goals you are striving for, your control and the success of the conference will be more assured.

2. Be warm in your presentation. A parent needs to feel that you are interested in his or her child. Beware of the human tendency to distort any situation—yours or that of the parents. Listen carefully to the parent's point of view. Right or wrong, it colors his actions and his reactions. Attempt to establish a climate where a parent can be as honest with you as possible, and does not have to be defensive about the home picture.

3. Take into account the needs of the parents and the pressures upon them when you make any decisions concerning their child. In your evaluation, consider the relationships between the child's needs, the school's needs, your needs, and the parent's needs.

4. Bear in mind that most parents are quite fearful of the authoritarian position of the school over their children. Defensively, they still remember their own school days, and their feelings that principals and teachers are never wrong. Parental hostility toward teachers of the past may easily be turned toward you, for no other reason than that a child frequently becomes the extension of the parent's personality. This hostility is difficult to accept. If possible, diplomatically point out what the parent appears to be doing, and stress the need for cooperation. Whether good or bad, many parents approach the school with the attitude that they are going to get for their children the things they never obtained for themselves: recognition, success, and attention.

5. At the conclusion of your conference, substantiate what happened by your notes. These additions will provide for better recall and later accurate evaluation if it becomes necessary.

6. Terminate the conference by offering at least one or two

concrete, positive, and practical suggestions that the parents can follow.

GUIDELINES TO ASSIST THE WILLING PARENT

When deciding upon the structure for your parent-teacher conference, work from the basic concepts that your "special case" needs help in strengthening his defense mechanisms—how he copes with himself as well as with those around him. The psyche of your "special case" may be positively reinforced with techniques such as the following.

Discuss with the parent the advantages that may accrue from giving the child specific responsibilities. These should be definitely in line with the child's masculine or feminine role. A boy should be given responsibilities that are similar to, and supervised by, the male parent figure. Similarly, a girl should be given feminine responsibilities likened to, and supervised by, the female parent figure. These responsibilities must be within the physical, mental, and emotional capabilities of the child. Success and completion are desired, not frustration and failure.

Stress the importance of consistency in parental behavior patterns toward a child. Consistency is an essential ingredient to any well-rounded living pattern, but to a growing child it is especially important in praise and punishment, standards of performance, and areas of responsibility.

A child is a human being, and reacts as such. It is essential that each child in the family feels he is treated equally. Equality does not necessarily mean that each child has the same amount of money spent on him or equal time with a parent; it means that his needs are as equally met as those of his siblings. Each child must feel that he has a somewhat equal opportunity to satisfy his needs, his desires, and his immediate goals.

Because every human being is different, it is necessary to help the parent accept the fact that his child functions at many and various levels. He may be emotionally five, chronologically seven, intellectually nine, and socially six. This is a very difficult concept for most parents to grasp. You, the wise teacher, will help the parent who is capable of helping his child to: a) explore the areas in which maturity is needed; and b) consider ways to assist the child to mature.

In the main, most parents are able to assimilate only one or two items from any individual parent-teacher conference. There is always value, when the need is present, to give specific homework or class assignments to the parent who is able and willing to help his child.

As an example, the weakest subject of one of your students who has become a "special case" is spelling. With outlined spelling assignments for the child and his parents to complete together, the child may respond very nicely. The real therapeutic value may be that the child-parent relationship becomes closer. Both child and parent often can accept and carry out daily assignments as a definite task toward helping the "special case." Unfortunately, this same family might be completely unable to act on a nebulous statement from a teacher who says "you and your child should do more things together."

Another, and less common, example of the second category of parents who can't or don't care is typified by Mr. Les D. He telephoned the principal's office following the teacher's third written request for a parent-teacher conference involving his daughter Emmy. Mr. D.'s conversation was short and final.

"I pay my taxes. I send my kids to school. It's your job to learn (sic) them. My wife and I are busy. We don't have time and we just don't care to hear anything about it. If my kids won't do what you tell them to at school, it's your job to take care of them. If you have any trouble with my kids, you straighten them out."

The principal thanked Mr. D. for his telephone call and made a note concerning the remarks for his record. Later that day, he spoke with Miss B., Emmy's teacher. As he suspected, Emmy was a "special case."

"What shall we do? I've been keeping records on Emmy and I feel her problem originates in her home."

To Miss B.'s dismay, her principal replied, "Well, this is one of the facts of life. A few parents, like Emmy's, just don't care about cooperating with the school. We will do the best we can."

Like Miss B., you the classroom teacher may be told in one way or another that there will be no support or cooperation from a child's parents. In spite of this you can still succeed with your "special case."

The third group of parents is exemplified by Mrs. K., whose two elementary school children have, for all practical purposes, reared themselves. Mrs. K. is forty-one, has divorced two husbands, and is currently interested in a twenty-four year old marine. Her oldest daughter, Karen (a fifth grader) was recognized as a "special case" almost as soon as the family moved into a new school district.

Requests for parent-teacher conferences were ignored repeatedly. Karen finally supplied the teacher with the explanation when she volunteered, "Mother just doesn't care. My sister and I have always taken care of ourselves. Mother has never come to school and she refuses to come now. She isn't interested in what happens to us."

Karen pinpointed a problem which every teacher must cope with. For one reason or another, many parents just don't really care what happens to their children. They refuse to help.

WHEN THE PARENT CANNOT OR WILL NOT HELP

With parents who, for one reason or another, cannot or refuse to help, the wise teacher will recognize that in counseling the child who has become a "special case," there are still many things to be done.

1 Face the facts of life. For innumerable reasons, some temporary, some permanent, there are parents who won't or who can't help their children. There are many who don't care what happens to their children insofar as the school situation is concerned.

2. Just because you get no cooperation from home does not mean that you will not succeed in returning your "special case" to normal. Utilize to the fullest, your bag of classroom tricks, your own ability at counseling, and the support provided by other students.

3. Explore all possible avenues of help from staff and school advisory personnel.

4. Confidence begets confidence. The teacher who believes that she can handle her "special cases" will succeed, with or without parental assistance.

5. Many times the teacher will be far more successful with the

"special case" when she has *no* parental help than she will in the case where the parents become actively involved, but subconsciously resist all that is being done.

6. If your "special case" has siblings in school, they may be a source of important information. If older, they may assume some of the parent figure role. If younger, they may supply you with answers. They may be part of the problem. More than one "special case" behavior pattern has returned to normal when his sibling relationships were readjusted.

7. Wise use of the mother and father image of the teacher and principal will work wonders in establishing stability for the child. Transference of a child's feelings to other parental figures is normal. When this transference occurs with strong positive figures who are consistent and supportive, a child always gains maturity.

8. Privileged information given to you, either by the child or by the parent, requires special handling. Beware of divulging, intentionally or unintentionally, such information.

Regardless of the amount of cooperation given by the parent, you the teacher are still the child's first line of support when he becomes a "special case." Your ability to function, in light of his individual needs and problems, may well be the key factor in whether this child returns to his normal behavior pattern or tends to drift toward becoming a chronic "special case." Time is always of the essence. The sooner you take positive action, whether or not the parent is involved, the more feasible and effective will be your solution.

CONSIDERATION FOR THE PEOPLE INVOLVED

Observe the behavior pattern of the parent and you will gain insight into that of the child. Every child is a product of his heredity and his environment. Even if you cannot arrange a contact with the parent, this fact of and by itself gives you information relating to the child's problem. There are many sources of information—records, administrators, specialists, previous teachers, and neighbors who also have children in your school. Listen!

A child is the product of his home. He may benefit from it or he may be victimized by it. Much of the action you take to help your "special case" will be based on how you evaluate the parent and sibling relationship in the home.

Whether you are able to work with them or not, never forget that parents are human beings. There is always a reason for what they do and why they do it. The parent or parent substitute is the first major influence on a child. Draw from this relationship to accomplish your goals.

The teacher who has compassion for parents and siblings as people can foster a similar compassion, undertanding, and acceptance on the part of the child.

It's always easy to pull a child's world out from under him. The capable teacher uses every positive value that the child has to build his ego and his defenses so that his feet will stay firmly on the ground.

6

Counseling the Normal Child Who Has Become a "Special Problem"

Those who teach must, of necessity, counsel.

"Dr. Miller, I'm losing control of my class. I feel my principal won't help me. Most of my students' parents won't help me. Each week I seem to have an additional problem child. In fact, most of the problem children appear to be getting worse."

Mr. Bob S., six-foot-two and twenty-eight, was normally the type of man considered outgoing, masculine, and self-assured. But when he came into my office, he had all the airs of defeat.

"I've been teaching the sixth grade for two and one half years in this system. Until just before Christmas I thought I was doing pretty well. And now, I feel certain I'm not going to get tenure."

"Why do you feel this way, Bob?"

"I thought I was hired to teach, and I'm prepared to teach. I know my subject thoroughly, but I'm just not prepared to be a nursemaid to a lot of problem kids. I want them out of my class. They belong in a special program somewhere, but my principal says I have to cope with them and teach them as best I can."

As a clinical psychologist, there was one thing only that I could tell him. "Bob, you're going to have to accept the harsh realities of your profession. The home is the most important single item in shaping the entire life of a child. Probably the second is the school. You, the teacher, are the parent figure at school. Your role, like that of the parent, involves most of the facets of a child's life when he is at school, and even some once he has left the school grounds. Every form of communication between the teacher and the pupil involves some form of counseling. Education is more than just book learning. You are trying to help your children find a way of life and to be successful in the society in which they find themselves.

"Furthermore, every teacher of an elementary child has to be a nursemaid of sorts. This is especially true in dealing with the problem child. There's no doubt, it's much easier to act as a nursemaid if you dignify the relationship of being a counselor."

It was some time before Bob could accept this broader concept of his role. When he was able to utilize some of the basic counseling techniques, he overcame many of his feelings of defeat. He received tenure on schedule, and became successful in his school system.

Like Bob, each elementary school teacher will have a certain percentage of "special cases," and will, of necessity, develop his own techniques to counsel them. Therefore, you the wise teacher, will be adaptable, flexible, and attuned to each "special case."

GUIDELINES TO KEEP IN MIND AS YOU COUNSEL

There is no question but that the guidelines, suggestions, and recommendations of this chapter are idealistic. In many instances, they are not realistic in view of the requirements and demands made upon the elementary school teacher. Time allotments in teacher schedules never really allow for adequate counseling of students. The many assigned academic disciplines to teach and the required administrative demands leave little leeway.

1. However, it must be recognized that first things often come first. If the discipline of the class is completely disruptive, little learning will be accomplished until stability is gained. If the children are hungry, diseased, or ill clothed, little learning will be accomplished until these primary needs are fulfilled. Likewise, if a child is emotionally upset or disturbed, the acquiring of academic knowledge will be minimal until he can adjust to himself and his environment

Fortunately, more and more elementary school districts are utilizing guidance counselors, teaching aids, assistants, and other means to resolve these problems. With such support, the conscientious teacher is able to find the minutes necessary to counsel her students.

2. Next to the parent and siblings in the home, you, the child's

teacher, are probably the most important factor in molding his psyche. When you counsel a child, you never know what may evolve. The situation that produces a "special case" may be temporary or chronic. Be prepared to constantly re-evaluate your counseling approaches and to shift your emphasis.

3. Physical and mental anomalies often create a "special case." Carefully ascertain whether or not such handicaps as poor hearing, inadequate eyesight, physical size, distortion or difference from the norm, malnutrition, or chronic illness play a part in the child's problem. Are these anomalies correctable or must the child learn to compensate for this loss? If there is a physical problem, involve the school nurse and medical authorities; a mental problem, the elementary guidance or curriculum personnel; an emotional problem, the psychological services.

4. Be prepared to meet any contingency. Attempt to understand the child's home environment, analyze what part this environment plays in the child's ability to cope with his school, as well as his personal problems.

5. Even though you may have some plan of referral in your school system, treat each "special case" (at least in the beginning of your counseling) as if you are the only available source of help.

6. Never forget that counseling, as opposed to discipline, is most effective if used after the individuals have "cooled-off." "Talking it out" verbally or ventilating your feelings to an empathetic listener is one of the most effective ways of setting the stage for emotional growth.

KNOW YOUR OWN LIMITATIONS

There are many inherent pitfalls for the teacher who is, of necessity, involved in counseling. Some of these were encountered by Mrs. Ann N., an experienced, conscientious third grade teacher who came to me for professional help because the pressures of her home, her administration, and her students, were creating too many personal tensions.

"Dr. Miller, where does teaching end, and counseling begin? I feel a moral obligation to help every child I have. And, like the Good Shepherd, I find myself urgently concerned whenever I have 'lost sheep' in class."

"What do you mean by 'lost sheep'?"

"Any child that has strayed, or is unable to get along with his peer groups or—oh, I mean just any child who is having trouble in school. I just simply have to do my best for him."

A few questions revealed that Mrs. N. was attempting too much. She identified with each student, and became so emotionally involved that she literally wore herself ragged. In fact, she experienced the feeling that she was the only Good Shepherd available to her students. She failed to utilize her school's chain of command, the child's parents, and the school resources at hand.

As her personal counseling continued, she was told "In the broadest analysis, you are literally over your head. You give yourself no break. Emotionally, you take all your student problems home with you every night, weekends, and vacations."

Furthermore, Mrs. N. was unaware of the extent of her capabilities to counsel. She attempted far more than she was qualified, or expected, to do. As she became aware of her capacity to handle her problem children, she increasingly took advantage of the resources around her. She limited her counseling to the areas in which she was effective and to school hours. With this subtle change, she was able to relax. "In fact," she said, "I made my own pressures. I was trying to remake the world all alone, I guess."

It is best to schedule counseling of students, whether individually or in groups, at a time when you are at your best emotionally, mentally, and physically. Whether male or female, we all have periods during which we tend to function better than others. For example, Miss Carol G., often considered her school's best fourth grade teacher, attempts to postpone counseling for the three-day period prior to the onset of her menstrual flow.

The ability to counsel will also be affected by such factors as age, experience, fatigue, and pressures emanating from social, economic, and physical stresses.

Naurally, children also have their cycles and their ups and downs. However, and for all practical purposes, you the teacher must set the stage for counseling when you feel it is indicated and you are most prepared to implement it.

SETTING THE STAGE FOR COUNSELING YOUR "SPECIAL CASE"

1. Choose the time when you are at your best, physically, mentally, and emotionally. Do not invite failure. Approach each "special case" positively and with confidence. Naturally, the more

experience you have, the more personal assuredness you will exhibit.

2. Marshall your previous experience with this type of "special case," and review possible courses of action. Familiarize yourself with whatever literature is available or with previous notes you may have recorded. If this is your first example of a particular type of "special case," recognize that you have to start some time. Prepare—then commence.

3. Consistently re-evaluate what you have done and what progress you have made. This should be in the form of a written progress report. Minimal notes are all that is necessary. As you re-evaluate, do not overlook the part played by physical problems, whether they are constant, changing, or intermittent. Poor hearing may be a constant problem. A broken leg or an increase in size may be a temporary physical factor to consider in your counseling approach.

4. When working with the "special case," remember you are riding a sort of "merry-go-round." If you don't catch the "brass ring," (the vital point of the problem), the first time around, you will the second or third time. One important point about counseling is that key elements of a problem keep reappearing. As you recognize them, you can cope with them.

5. Take as much advantage as possible of the support you can enlist from other students, the siblings and parents of the "special case," teachers, administrators, school consultants, and resource materials (such as you find in the chapters of this book).

6. Ideas, concepts, guidelines, and techniques are only tools. It is necessary for you to arrange them to fit your needs and the demands of counseling your "special case."

7. Accept the fact that the authorities in the field are able to talk, or write, only in terms of general procedures that may apply to many cases. Seldom, if ever, will these specialists give you such definite recommendations for counseling that they will pertain to every specific "special problem." Yet, the broad information that they give provides the basis for selecting and perfecting your own personal tools and techniques.

8. Each situation will be unique. Even though you may have the same set of circumstances, tomorrow will be different from today. As an example, today may be rainy and tomorrow the sun may shine. Today your "special case" may be on the playground with five peers. Tomorrow there may be six peers. Today he may have

had a good breakfast. Tomorrow he may have had little to eat before he came to school. Each of many physical, emotional, environmental, and mental factors will affect your case and its outcome.

PLAYING YOUR ROLE BY EAR

The successful counselor, in spite of all his knowledge and experience, "plays his role by ear," using all the intuition that the Good Lord gave him.

Each of us who goes into the field of professional education will expect to encounter and solve problems involved in helping his students who have become "special cases." This is especially true in the early years of your career as you gain teaching experience. It is not inconceivable that, in the course of his elementary school training, every child at one time or another becomes a "special case." Therefore, the wise teacher is alert to the immediate changes in each child's behavior patterns. He is aware too that any individual, situation or condition, or a series or combination of these, may produce the "special case."

The case history of Willy is a good example. He came to school Thursday morning obviously worried, upset, and fearful. During the early morning, he continued to distract the students around him. This behavior pattern was abnormal for him, in that he was usually calm and was not considered a disruptive force in the classroom.

Miss R., Willy's third grade teacher, knew that discipline in the form of punishment would force Willy to be quiet or sit still. However, being attuned to the child's needs, she decided to spend the time to find out the reason the boy was upset. Willy, at this point, certainly wasn't a "special case," but he needed her help. During recess, Miss R. talked with him and discovered that the previous evening he had been left alone with a baby sitter. He had watched a television movie that involved the destruction of the world. Lacking complete comprehension and basically insecure, Willy had personalized this movie. He told Miss R., "I'm going to lose everybody. We're all going to die. That's what it said on T.V."

Quickly Miss R. explained, "This was a movie. It's only a story; it isn't necessarily true. Our world isn't going to end. Let's enjoy life today. You were here yesterday and you will probably be here tomorrow. If this type of movie upsets you, Willy, don't stay up and watch. Now let's go out to recess and have fun."

Several times during the afternoon Miss R. gave Willy additional reassurance. A potential problem was eliminated. The next day Willy was his usual cheerful self. Once a threatening situation or condition is removed or alleviated, a child tends to return to normal, as did this boy.

With most children, therapeutically oriented counseling is apt to get positive results far more rapidly than with adults. Very often a child with a specific set of neuroses may respond favorably to a minimal change in emotional, social, or physical environment. An adult, on the other hand, with a similar syndrome, especially one that has been reinforced over many years, may require considerable professional treatment to make this same adjustment.

Take the case of Linda, who would be considered a "special case" (whereas Willy was not). Linda was in the fourth grade and rather withdrawn from the world of reality. Frequently she verbalized fantasies of being an important figure. Clearly, this child showed slight schizophrenic tendencies. At this point she would not be diagnosed as a schizophrenic, but her present neurosis, with a potential of becoming a psychosis, may well be pinpointed and helped. Linda was fortunate in that her teacher, Mrs. Phyllis J., was able to provide a minimal change in the child's environment in school. Through personal warmth, she drew Linda into group participation. In the same manner, Mrs. J., as she listened, was able to counsel Linda in her verbalized stories to recognize that much was fantasy and wishful thinking, rather than reality.

Linda became more realistic; she participated with her group. Her schizophrenic tendencies were subdued. Mrs. J.'s counseling did not resolve a permanent problem, but it enabled Linda to develop a set of defense mechanisms which served her temporarily. Strengthened sufficiently, these mechanisms may very well last her a lifetime. Had she not had counseling by Mrs. J. or a person in a similar role, Linda's potential toward schizophrenia would, in all probability, have increased.

If the conditions surrounding any child are too catastrophic, and he cannot adjust to them, even with the use of professional help, he may have to be physically removed from his immediate society before his behavior pattern will tend to return to normal. Stephen was a good example of just such a change in environment. He lived in a home where extreme physical violence was the rule. At school he had been the center of continual physical and verbal arguments. The situation deteriorated to the point where Stephen was sent to live in a foster home. There the environment provided warmth instead of hatred, consistency instead of irregularity, and security instead of instability. Stephen's aggressive actions decreased and he was able to adjust to the school in the district of his foster home with minimal difficulties.

Once this pattern of warmth, consistency, and security has been established, the "special case," like Stephen, tends to return to normal. There are rare exceptions, of course, where the child becomes extremely neurotic or psychotic, and needs extensive professional, or even institutional, care.

It's important that you, the teacher, be extremely aware of your limitations in the areas of counseling the "special case." You are not a psychiatrist nor a psychologist. Do not try to be one!

Of necessity, you will use many of the tools used by professional therapists, but if you use them within the scope of your own abilities and experience, you will be effective and will accomplish your goals. When you have a problem case that goes beyond your capabilities, admit it. Accept the fact that you can't handle it alone. Refer it.

Children are miniature adults, even more susceptible than their older counterparts to the internal and external stresses and the pressures of their society. It is not easy to identify the child who is having difficulty coping effectively with his world.

IDENTIFYING THE EMERGING "SPECIAL CASE"

• Watch for changing behavior patterns which may indicate a child in trouble. For example, Jimmy has been friendly, happy, and outgoing with his classmates. Suddenly, he becomes moody, unhappy, and withdrawn. Perhaps Jimmy is becoming a "special case."

• What appears to be generating his personality change? Does it originate from inward or outward sources?

• When are the personality changes most evident?

• Why are these changes occurring? Look first to the child's own world, then to outside factors that might be responsible—parents, siblings, peers, yourself, others in authority.

• Where are the changes to be seen—playground, classroom, to and from school, home, other?

- Are these changes affecting the child, and how do they occur?
- Pinpoint the types of behavior patterns you observe and keep a written record of what appears to be happening and what you feel may be the problem. What are his responses to your various methods and techniques of discipline, control, and motivation?

COMMUNICATION—A BASIC TOOL IN COUNSELING

Effective communication forms a firm base on which a child can develop socially acceptable behavior patterns. I think probably the most important, perhaps the single, concept in counseling any child, is to remember: Every form of communication involving the teacher and her pupils is potential counseling. This counseling is done along with teaching, discipline, and other interpersonal relationships developed in the classroom and on the playground. It is true whether you are working with a child as an individual, the individual as one of a group, or the group as an integral unit.

Communication utilizes all of the senses. It is a two-way street. It involves the teacher and it involves the child. Both must give as well as receive. For instance, if a teacher only talks and does not listen, she has no way of determining whether her students understand her, or are even on the same wave length. Without a constant verbal and activity feedback from each student, it is highly possible that there has been little or no communication.

The same is true with all the other senses. Teachers, as well as pupils, react to each and every internal and external stimulus, whether it is a sonic boom, someone walking by the window, a tummy ache, or one of a thousand other things. The communication process is affected by practically everything in the home, school, or community environment. The wise teacher uses as many stimuli, from as many sources as possible, to strengthen communication and to give a potential problem child insight into his feelings. She helps him learn what may be done and in what ways he may do it to satisfy his personal and individual needs.

For example, Frank finishes his work quickly and then proceeds to annoy everyone around him by whispering, poking, or throwing pieces of paper. Frank is an increasingly disruptive force in the classroom. Too frequently, those in authority will handle Frank's problem by standing him in the corner, isolating him from the group, or sending him to the principal. These forms of discipline are often temporarily helpful, but offer little long-range value because they do not deal with the reasons for the behavior. How much time you have available to cope with the problem is always a critical factor. For Frank's sake, it is probably preferable to design a counseling situation enabling him to become aware of the unpleasantness he is causing. In this particular incident, Frank's fifth grade teacher, Mr. William Y., took the latter course of action. He counseled Frank and gave him increased responsibility, a positive form of self-discipline. He assigned Frank as a monitor for one week, promising additional roles of leadership, if Frank could convince him he was "man enough for the job." The appeal to the boy's need to be important was well-founded, and he was handled in a socially acceptable manner. In the course of his duties, Frank recognized in the conduct of his peers, his own disruptive behavior patterns. This was especially true when such behavior patterns were verbally and dramatically interpreted for the class by his teacher.

Mr. Y. utilized subtle group and individual counseling techniques and thus achieved four goals. First, he used discipline, but avoided inflicting pain upon Frank; second, he gave Frank, as a person and as a human being, verbal and physical approval; third, he pinpointed the fact that Frank was a normal child who had developed into a "special case," and in so doing he took positive counseling steps to solve the problem; fourth, he gave the entire class, and especially Frank, insight and support within a learning situation. Counseling such as was used by Mr. Y., involves insight, interpretation, permissiveness, and support, all tempered by love.

As a clinical psychologist, I believe that there are certain fundamentals in counseling that, if followed by a teacher, will produce desired results with almost any "special case" in the school situation. In addition, when a child becomes a "special case" that requires more than the teacher can give, I believe that the teacher is still the key member of the professional team that may be called upon to treat the child needing psychotherapy. In a large number of incidents, the alert teacher makes the initial recommendations that lead to adequate professional help for the acutely neurotic or psychotic child. The teacher's notes and reports certainly become the basis for further professional referral and therapy.

Fortunately, you will discover that the vast majority of your "special cases" will respond positively to the counseling that falls within the limits of your capabilities.

GUIDELINES FOR COUNSELING YOUR "SPECIAL CASE"

1. If you are a teacher, you are a counselor.
2. Nearly every form of communication between the teacher and pupil will involve counseling.
3. Be alert to the fact that every child may possibly, at some time, become a "special case."
4. As you counsel, accept the realities of your capacities and of the child's potential. Try to specifically delineate these capacities and potentials.
5. You will be effective in counseling only if you work within the scope of your own abilities and experience, whether these are limited or extensive.
6. Analyze what goals you are trying to accomplish and how effective you are. Use the checklists (see the Appendix) to determine what counseling is indicated and how you can implement it. There will be a record of your progress; where you were successful and where you failed.
7. Never underestimate the good that you can accomplish. Fortunately, the human child is able to withstand what often appears to be insurmountable emotional and physical depravation, and ill-treatment, and yet respond extremely well to a small amount of warm and supportive understanding.
8. A child tends to speak in his own language, and in terms of his own comprehension of the world around him. It is difficult, if not almost impossible, for an adult to really return to a child's level. However, if you are attuned to this reality of a child's life, your effectiveness as a counselor is usually high.
9. Let the child talk. Listen with warmth and an open understanding. Possibly the child will resolve much of his problem by bringing it into the open. Often, routine information or a slight interpretation will help him to resolve the difficulty.
10. Never close the door on a child's opportunity to achieve and to understand himself.

7

Little Attention Getters

*All the world's a stage. Every child
has a right to center stage.*

Every normal child wants and needs attention, especially from you, his teacher. Thus, you can anticipate continuous competitive striving from each child for your personal attention. Symptoms of this striving include practically every conceivable defense mechanism and "attention getting" technique that is possible at the conscious, as well as the subconscious level. Therefore, you will find it necessary to cope constantly with the normal child's attention needs.

GUIDELINES TO CONTROL "ATTENTION GETTING" MECHANISMS OF THE NORMAL CHILD

1. Accept the fact that "attention getting" is a normal mechanism of every individual.

2. Provide daily, and if possible in the very first hour, an opportunity for each child to get some individual attention. This may be done simply by physically patting each child, shaking his hand, talking to him directly, or letting him know that you feel his presence and importance.

3. Remember that most children need to be recognized, consistently and frequently. Develop daily opportunities for such recognition of each child. Use the child's name and his accomplishments.

4. Help every one of your students to gain awareness as to when and how he receives love. Love is the most important force in shaping a child's life.

51

5. If a child is newly enrolled, has been absent, or for any other reason appears to need positive attention, he may be singled out in a friendly, specific manner, or be given first turn in any exercise.

For example, Johnny, a second grader, has been absent. On his return, and within the first five minutes of calling the class to order, Miss L. says, "Johnny has been sick with a bad cold and has been gone all week. Let's all clap and show him how glad we are to have him back with us today." This public recognition goes a long way toward overcoming Johnny's feelings of being forgotten. He knows that he is still one of the group and is loved by his teacher. This consideration by Miss L. increases Johnny's desire to be in school and is a positive factor toward any child's recovery from illness.

6. Normal "attention getting" needs may be satisfied by a "sharing time" when every child is invited to verbally, and at times physically, share what he feels is important. Make liberal use of class procedures which allow the children to take turns. You will then be able to say, as did a recently retired and gifted elementary teacher, "Whenever I've had troubled students demanding excessive attention, I've promptly turned the class session into a sharing one. Whether it involves speaking about experiences, writing, or drawing pictures, I feel this use of sharing tends to smooth out the disruption, and to make each child feel he is getting his share of attention."

7. Control the physical environment for the benefit of the class as well as yourself. Change the seating, the blackboard arrangements, the assignments, and the playground areas to fit the continually changing needs of the individual student, the class, and the faculty.

8. Beware of "pets." Everyone of us likes a good student, and there is a strong tendency when we personally are in need of support to turn to the student who will give such support in the form of a right answer. Even though this child may be the "sharpest" in class, he or she may subtly use this technique to gain attention. Draw out responses from others, even when they aren't sure of the correct answers.

9. In the same light, be cognizant of the class "idol," the counterpart of "teacher's pet," who, with the same degree of subtlety, uses the class because of his special abilities, athletic skill, physical power, brains, family prestige, or status, to produce a favorable

environment in which he fulfills his own excessive attention needs. By indirectly building the classroom and playground status of others to equal that of the "idol," you will dissipate the problem.

10. Provide varied opportunities for each student to play a leading role in some situation. Set up a workable schedule that allows a period of time for each one to perform his role. Allow the child to proceed from beginning to end, regardless of how inept he may be. Once you establish a schedule, carry it out.

11. Note that a child who needs attention will do anything, positively or negatively, to gain it, and thus satisfy his needs. You may be fulfilling his need through scolding, ridiculing, or spankings. When you provide him such satisfaction, you may work to the detriment of the child, as well as the school situation.

12. Unfortunately, pain is still the quickest teacher. There are some children, and some situations, for which negative action forms the most feasible solution. However, pain should be administered only in conformity with approved school and district procedures, and in close cooperation with your administrators.

EVALUATING THE COURSES OF ACTION

When the normal guidelines, as given above, fail, you may have a situation needing additional positive action. Begin by evaluating your students. Single out the potential "special case" by using the following four steps:

- Be aware of the characteristics of the "special case."
- Proceed step by step to delineate the problem.
- Choose a course of action which you, the teacher, and your administration may find effective in resolving the "special case."
- Analyze the possible procedures you will follow if referral is needed.

THE CHARACTERISTICS OF THE "SPECIAL CASE"

Once you decide that you have a "special case," or a possible "special case," involving the normal child striving for excessive attention, the main decision confronting you is:

"How do I recognize not just the symptoms of the problem, or even the problem itself, but the characteristics of the particular 'special case' needing my personal help?"

It is important to remember that in "attention getting," as with so many other "special case" problems, what may appear to be a serious psychological problem is actually the outgrowth of the normal expected characteristics, irritants, antagonisms, etc., which any child has. Usually a child's behavior patterns are controlled through discipline and other normal classroom techniques and do not become a problem. The "special case" appears when these normal techniques lose their effectiveness or do not produce the desired results. This child then needs additional attention, support, guidance, and help, in order that he may replace his unacceptable behavior patterns with ones that are acceptable. Realistically, he is not an emotionally disturbed child in need of psychotherapy, but a child who is emotionally, physically, and mentally inadequately adjusting to his school environment. He needs your counseling to help resolve the problems that make him a "special case."

Tommy is a "special case." He is short, wears poor clothes, and comes from a low income home. Since the beginning of the semester, his teacher has used the normal techniques to satisfy his needs for attention, and to utilize his contributions in class. They have not been effective. Tommy's appetite is insatiable.

To enhance his status as a disruptive force in the classroom, he continues to bring to school live frogs, toads, snakes, and lizards. When he exhibits them, he accomplishes three important goals:

1. He gets positive attention from his masculine peers. They side with him in the disturbance. They identify with him as a leader, and may follow his example by bringing to school similar "class disrupting" material.

2. He gets heterosexual attention and enjoyment from his female peers. They react in feminine ways. They may act negatively and scream and run, but may still be attracted to Tommy. They may act positively and accept Tommy as their masculine leader. They may even partially or completely reject him.

3. He gets negative attention from you, the teacher, in the form of lack of approval or disciplinary action.

In each of these instances, Tommy fulfills his needs and what he wants, attention, is gotten. It is excessive, both negative and positive, individual and group. Tommy has momentarily at least, assumed control of the class. This need to grasp control, in opposition to the desire of the teacher, is a characteristic of many normal children who strive for excessive attention.

Why, then, is a child like Tommy a "special case"? How do you recognize the symptoms exhibited when a child is becoming a "special case"? And what are the general characteristics of the "special case"? In attempting to satisfy his excessive attention needs, the "special case" child may exhibit positive behavior patterns. He may:

- Demand that he be watched.
- Interrupt and force others to listen to what he says.
- Assume the guilt of others and direct disciplinary action toward himself.
- Pressure those about him to act as he does, or to do what he wants done.
- Arrive early and stay late.

In addition, he may exhibit negative and indirect techniques. He may:

- Whine excessively.
- Complain about being hurt or "picked on."
- Arrive late and want to leave early.
- Do the opposite of what is expected of him.
- Loiter on the way home.
- Refuse to eat, answer questions, and participate in school activities.

All of these, and similar "attention getting" mechanisms may be considered perfectly normal, provided the child responds to the usual techniques of discipline, and provided such behavior patterns are used infrequently.

GUIDELINES FOR PINPOINTING THE CHARACTERISTICS OF THE "SPECIAL CASE"

You will recognize the developing "special case" child when he exhibits both of the following characteristics:

1. He has sufficient command of his techniques to take the control of the classroom or the playground situation away from the designated authority figure.

2. He exhibits a quality of "moreness." He is louder than those around him. He does more to try the patience of the teacher and

the class. He incites more behavior problems in his peers as he develops opportunities to perfect his techniques. He is involved in increasingly more disciplinary action.

DETERMINING TO WHAT EXTENT A CHILD IS BECOMING A "SPECIAL CASE"

When more and more characteristics of a "special case" appear in one of your students, proceed step by step to delineate the problem. Use your checklists in this delineation. As you gain more and more experience in counseling specific types of "special cases," you will find it most effective to develop your own checklists. (See Appendix for examples of formats for such possible checklists that would apply to problems of "attention getting.")

As you record your observations, you have a written and comparable record available to you in your decision making. Is this particular child who now is, or is becoming a "special case," actually a problem arising from a demand for excessive attention?

Does the problem involve only one "special case," such as Tommy? Are other class members involved? Does the one "special case" trigger off all of the excessive attention demands? Do the problems show that additional "special cases" exist? Are your normal patterns of class control and disciplinary techniques becoming less effective?

To answer these questions, use your checklists. Through them you may move, step by step, to pinpoint the "special cases" and to delineate the extent of the problem.

HOW TO HANDLE THE CHILD WHO HAS BECOME A "SPECIAL CASE"

Automatically, as one pupil's "attention getting" patterns become a problem, you will begin to use accepted positive and negative techniques to keep this disruptive force in the classroom within normal acceptable limits. How then, do you determine when the routine disciplining techniques are failing you? Appraise your corrective actions. Are they getting the results you desire? Does one technique appear more useful than another? Are you satisfying the child's needs in such a way that you are increasing or decreasing the "attention getting" problem? What actually is happening?

Ten year old Janice O. is a "special case" of "attention getting."

She is a fourth grade student and, although from a moderately well-to-do income group, she receives little or no attention in her home surroundings. At school, Janice soon discovered that her teacher, Miss E., could be counted on to give her the attention she craved. This attention was negative and painful, but to the child it partially filled a deep void. Every time Janice created a disturbance, Miss E. applied a negative form of discipline. The more frequently Janice misbehaved, the more negative attention Miss E. gave her. Unconsciously, the teacher nourished the child's need for painful attention. By the time the principal became aware of the situation, the disruptive force in the class was so great that it was necessary to transfer the child to another fourth grade teacher.

Had Miss E. recognized that her discipline was ineffective and merely increased the problem, and had she been able to supply the child's attention needs in constructive class-oriented outside projects, the problem would very possibly have resolved itself. As in the example of Janice, such problems frequently arise because the child's excessive attention needs could be, but are not met in the school situation in a positive, socially acceptable manner.

GUIDELINES AS YOU COUNSEL THE CHILD WHO HAS BECOME A "SPECIAL CASE"

• Compromise between the various needs that are in evidence in your class. Be aware that you, the teacher, are intent on covering a certain amount of material. Each child is intent on satisfying his needs

• Be flexible enough to interrupt a pre-planned program to solve immediately a child's "attention getting" needs. A few minutes at the right time may save frustrating hours later.

• Allow the child to state his needs. Give him opportunity to ventilate his feelings. There are many times when counseling can't be done in a group or before the class, but will best be accomplished in private at a later time.

• Show the child that he, in reality, is receiving attention. Point out where it comes from, and how it can and does satisfy his personal needs. This may be done verbally or through activities in the classroom and playground situation.

There is much that the classroom teacher, working alone, can accomplish through indirect and direct counseling.

The indirect method is conducted in such a way that the child and the class in general are unaware of what the teacher is doing. The indirect method may be both positive and negative.

For example, it's baseball time. Timothy has been consistently elbowing everybody out of the way to get attention. He is not a "special case," but unless this normal drive is met and channeled into acceptable outlets, a "special case" could develop.

The playground supervisor, aware of this problem, says, "Timothy, select the players for one team and then choose who will play each position." When the selections have been made, the supervisor continues, "Now, Timothy, you are the manager and score keeper. Sit at the table by the bench and start keeping score."

Very subtly, and in this positive manner, the teacher feeds Timothy's ego by making him the center of attraction. Yet, at the same time, she forces Timothy to recognize the importance of others as he chooses them to assume major roles. Furthermore, she has removed Timothy from center stage and given equal recognition to others. Training, teaching, and counseling are all involved.

Likewise, in the classroom, and using the indirect approach, a teacher can specifically single out a child needing attention. In order to make him important in the eyes of the whole class, assign him a project on which to report.

Kathy, although the smallest girl in the class and a physically handicapped child, is also the smartest. She has recently returned from a summer vacation trip to several of the national parks. Incessantly, she is whispering or getting the attention of others by retelling her travels. Her instructor, Miss Jones, sensing Kathy's need for attention, immediately tells the class, "On Friday morning at ten o'clock, Kathy will have a half hour period during which to report on her trip to the national parks." Then she addresses Kathy, "Bring in descriptive pictures, maps, and literature which you have collected during the summer." With this positive commitment, she effectively concludes, "Kathy, you are not to talk again in class about your trip until Friday." This indirect counseling satisfies Kathy's needs, and at the same time, returns order to the classroom situation.

John F., a fifth grader, talks continuously and disrupts everyone around him. Mr. Elmer G., his teacher, having had this same trouble previously with John, simply walks to the back of the room and, with his forefinger, snaps John on the top of the head. John yelps, "Ow!" Then Mr. G. informs John and the whole class, "There will be no more of this disturbance and talking." There is none.

Caught by surprise as Mr. G. uses his direct disciplinary action, a negative pain technique, the class returns to order. At the end of the period, Mr. G., having set the scene to his liking, continues handling John's problem with a positive and direct counseling approach. He talks to John alone, on a man-to-man basis, about his behavior in class, the problems it creates, and what John may or may not do about it. Mr. G. also explains what his and the school's course of action will be if John can't control and change his behavior pattern.

Such direct and indirect techniques can and should be used almost continuously with various students during every class and recess period. They're effective with a child who may become a "special case," as well as one who already has become one.

• De-sensitize the feelings that are forcing the "special case" to seek attention. These feelings may include fears, anxieties, guilt, hostility, and frustrations. Talk about these feelings and the needs to accept and understand them. Act them out in classroom role playing. At any event, bring them out into the open and allow the child to become aware that they exist and that, per se, they are not wrong. It's how we handle our feelings that counts.

• Help the child to face reality as it exists. Fortunately, or unfortunately, there are times, such as during a fire drill, when conformity is urgent and attention cannot be given to the individual. Similarly, there are situations, such as being given the star role in a play, in which the child can attain an excessive amount of attention in a socially acceptable manner.

As each child matures, your opportunities to use verbalization, both in a directive and nondirective way, will increase. Often it is convenient to sit down alone with the child and realistically discuss the problem as you see it. Allow the student to talk about the problems as he sees them. Communications require giving and taking, talking and listening. His verbalizations, if you are really able to listen to them, will give you clues to his problems and in many instances, will help him resolve them.

• Decide whether discipline becomes more effective if the whole class is made aware that a problem exists.

For instance, Mrs. E. finds that three girls and two boys in her fifth grade class are constantly passing notes and talking. She tries direct discipline with minimal effect. Evaluating the problems involved, she decides on a more subtle approach. She applies the principle of "peer sanction." Quietly, but firmly, she presents her decision, "We must have a learning situation that is free of confusion. The whole class will stay after school today for ten minutes. All of you will make up the time lost during this period, due to the noise and disruption of the 'attention getting' five."

After school, in a group counseling situation, she asks for and receives the reactions of the class to the problems and possible solutions. Mrs. E. does not name names, but the social pressure is sufficient to curb the extent of this behavior problem for several days.

• Recognize that one technique, or one form of control, can never be counted on to be effective continuously. The wise teacher will have available a whole repertoire of guidelines to aid in coping with the "special case" striving for excessive attention.

• Be prepared to counsel with the child on a more formal basis if necessary. This may be done privately and at a convenient time selected to provide an atmosphere conducive to mutual problem solving. Follow through with the child's parents at their usual parent-teacher conference. You are concerned with the whole child, how he functions in his entire environment, how he satisfies his needs, and how he protects himself. The more you know about him, the more effective your counseling will be.

• Review your written evaluations of the child's behavior patterns periodically. Use checklists that you feel are tailored to your needs. An occasional problem may be disregarded, but the evidence of "moreness" must be heeded.

• Keep a resume based upon your observations, evaluations, and summaries from your checklists. This resume will provide an excellent basis for preparing material for use in conjunction with your regularly scheduled parent-teacher conferences.

One of the significant values of such a continuing resume of behavior patterns is that it establishes a written record that can be used by teacher, principal, Pupil Personnel specialists, or other professional referral sources when needed in determining disposition of any case. This resume pinpoints areas in which the problem may originate—home, school, playground, or in the individual's own personality. With it, you will be in a better position to discover clues as to the interrelationship of the child's various behavior patterns. Such a periodic resume should be kept in conjunction with the daily attendance and grade report. It must not become a part of the official records, but is still available to all concerned.

Your resume of any emerging "special case" may give you "center stage" when you need it. Also for your "special case" in "attention getting," this resume may well be an important aid in revealing clues of other emotional needs.

POSITIVE GUIDELINES CONCERNING REFERRALS

Referral is, basically, an admission of defeat. But you, as a wise teacher, must recognize that with some problem children you must accept this temporary defeat if your overall classroom work is to prosper. Too often, a good teacher feels that it is imperative to be successful with every student, and that he or she must solve every problem. However, before your "special case" becomes such a disruptive force in your classroom that your learning situation gets completely out of hand, seek administrative assistance.

If the child's problem continues to become more acute, be prepared to take positive action. Severity of the problem is often a matter of degree evaluated by the teacher and administrator through observation and testing. Do not hesitate to start the necessary "ball rolling" to enlist the advice and facilities of the school or other professional resources available to you, and in a position to aid the child.

A properly designed and maintained checklist, with a periodic summary or resume, will be helpful in giving you the information needed concerning the progress of the case, the type of action needed, who may be involved, pending disposition, and other pertinent information which might be made available to you concerning the referral. Consistent use of selected and well kept checklists will supply you with a firm basis for the direct and indirect counseling you do. In addition, they will aid you in any decisions you take in referring your "special cases," if and when such referral becomes necessary.

WHEN A "SPECIAL CASE" SHOULD BE REFERRED

With the checklists you find most effective, use the positive guidelines in reaching a decision to refer your "special case" to your school special services facilities or other sources of professional help. These guidelines are valid for each of the "special cases" evaluated and analyzed in this book.

1. Never underestimate the problem of excessive "attention getting." Unless resolved, it is normally a spreading one. It may increase in individual students, as well as an entire class. It may be teacher-oriented, school-oriented, or community-oriented as a problem. If you have reason to believe from your evaluations that the problem is increasing, consult your principal and available school specialists for possible solutions.

2. Recognize that you teach for the greatest number of students and that the individuals at each end of the normal distribution curve may need help that, for any number of reasons, you are unable to give.

3. Remember that progress in counseling your "special case" is best accomplished with empathy, not sympathy. Understand the child and his problems, and you can maintain a professional position of emotional uninvolvement. When you become personally involved in the child's problems, and sympathize with him or identify with him, your effectiveness in direct or indirect counseling diminishes. Emotional detachment is essential for effective, unbiased referrals on a professional basis.

4. When the resolution of the problems of your "special case" appears to be getting further and further away, and your difficulties with the child continue to increase, accept the reality that you are not succeeding. Starting with your principal, request the advice and the assistance of the school and community resources available to you. Do everything within your power to enable the child to take advantage of any school or community facilities for children with emotional handicaps.

8

Little Retreaters

*A child does not live in a world
alone. He lives in a world of people.*

Most children, in one way or another, frequently withdraw—
emotionally, mentally, or physically—from both the classroom and
the playground. In fact, during various times of the day, every
normal elementary class will have many incidents of temporary
withdrawing. Either as individuals or even in small groups, your
students sit lost in their thoughts, get up to sharpen pencils, look
out the window, go to the bathroom, or move in other distracting
patterns that are a form of withdrawal.

To a lesser degree, these and other similar behavior patterns
continually occur on the playground and throughout the school.
There, a boy or girl may want to play alone or with only one friend.
He may partially or completely isolate himself.

Like "attention getting," behavior patterns of withdrawal are
developed and used as defenses by every child. Through these patterns he is able, temporarily or permanently, to achieve three goals:

1. Satisfy many of his basic drives and desires. This may be
   done either positively or negatively.
2. Protect his psyche.
3. Defend himself against real or imaginary hurts.

Like any animal, a child, when hurt, tends to withdraw and lick
his wounds. The adage, "for he that fights and runs away, may live
to fight another day," applies to all of us.[1]

---

[1] Burton Stevenson, *Home Book of Proverbs, Maxims, and Familiar Phrases*
(New York: Macmillan Company, 1948), p. 801.

However, licking wounds is not the only reason a child withdraws. There may be a real need to gain perspective on relationships with his environment. For example, in order to attack a problem from a new approach, he may consciously or subconsciously desire time to wait until the physical, emotional, or mental climate changes.

Jack, for instance, has sat concentrating for nearly half an hour. Physically and mentally he needs to get away from his chair, as well as the arithmetic problem he has been unable to solve. He gets up twice to sharpen his pencil. Mrs. Thomas, his teacher, says, "Jack, that pencil's already sharp." Jack withdraws, stops working, and subconsciously looks at the situation. Instinctively, he needs to get out of his seat. He asks to be excused to go to the bathroom. When he returns, he is able to cope with the situation. A normal type of withdrawal has served Jack well.

Retreat from a momentarily intolerable situation is desirable. In fact, it supplies subconscious strength in the following ways:

- Helps the child to build up, or reconstruct, his ego defenses.
- Keeps the child from being additionally hurt
- Often is a technique to gain support from peers as well as from seniors.

However, withdrawal usually offers only a temporary solution to a child's problems. Used with increasing frequency, withdrawal tends toward the abnormal, and the child becomes a "special case."

Excessive retreat may be found in the neurotic who has become a hermit, or in the psychotic who has become a schizophrenic.

GUIDELINES TO CONTROL WITHDRAWAL PATTERNS IN THE NORMAL CHILD

1. Recognize that at times, every one of us must withdraw when a situation becomes too threatening or too hurtful.

2. Allow each child the opportunity to withdraw at least for a minimal time without questioning his reasons.

3. Every child has a secret world into which he may withdraw to lick his wounds, or to escape from something he does not wish to face or do. In general, he needs at this time to flee the realities of life. Such hiding may be constructive or destructive, but it is necessary for his psychic survival

4. Withdrawal patterns may be well handled through ignoring them, provided that:

a) They are not interfering with the child's learning pattern.

b) They are not affecting his social and interpersonal relationships in the classroom and on the playground.

c) They remain relatively consistent and normally stable for him.

d) They are not disruptive to the class and school social situation.

5. When the ignoring technique fails, verbally call attention to the child and/or the class. This may very well snap the child out of such patterns, especially if they involve daydreaming, looking out the window, or physically isolating himself by doodling, reading unrelated material, or actually leaving the class.

6. If a large percentage of, or the entire class membership itself, adopts withdrawal patterns, seek an immediate and specific reason.

For example, it may be a hot day, uncomfortable for studying. The subject material may be uninteresting. Perhaps a possible crisis is worrying all the students. The hurt of a child during the previous recess, or a community activity which has everyone preoccupied, may be the causal factor of the class's need to withdraw.

Group counseling that involves the ventilating of a few children's feelings may return the whole class to normal.

7. If a normally outgoing child suddenly adopts one or more patterns of withdrawal, talk with the child individually. Attempt to pinpoint the reason and to desensitize the fears and hurts he may be experiencing.

Both of Bobby's parents are flying on a convention trip and he is afraid they will be killed in a crash and he will be left alone. Personal reassurance from you, his teacher, may help him to more adequately cope with his fears until the return of his parents.

Another example of similar anxiety-producing situations arises when a baby is born into the household, when a brother or sister is sick, when there is an anticipated event (such as going to tne circus), or when the Little League ball teams are being chosen.

Such situations, plus the numerous other normal events in the life of a child, offer excellent opportunities for your counseling. Guide each child in his decision to put "first things first," as you stress the importance of carrying out the normal classroom and playground routines.

8. Some forms of withdrawal by the normal child may be best handled through positive disciplinary action. This is especially true in instances such as:

    a) The intellectually oriented child who withdraws by reading books or by refusing to participate in class.

    b) The athletic child who won't come in from playing ball.

    c) The relatively anti-social or non-conforming child who plays truant to get away from the school or home situation.

9. By and large, most withdrawal patterns adopted by the normal child do not respond favorably to punishment In fact, even positive discipline may increase the problem, forcing the child into more severe withdrawal symptoms, such as running away, hiding, or completely emotionally isolating himself.

The wise teacher will be careful in the use of any discipline, positive or negative, in instances of temporary withdrawal.

EVALUATING THE COURSES OF ACTION

• It is well to remember that the positive guidelines listed above are not designed to pinpoint the "special case." They are effective, however, in helping both the child who is a "special case," as well as the child who is not, to control and direct in an acceptable pattern his needs to withdraw. It is easy to brand (label) a normal child as a "special case" simply because he has a series of temporary situations to meet, and meets them through withdrawal techniques. Label a child as a "special case" only after careful evaluation.

• It is often most effective to accept and to tolerate withdrawal patterns. They are normal, and frequently are the easiest way for a child to protect himself from immediate, and to him, catastrophic problems. He frequently will find a more acceptable defense if left to himself.

• Use your checklists to aid you in determining whether a child is becoming a "special case," and needs your additional help.

• Tendencies toward extreme neuroses or psychoses are not easily delineated. Therefore, the wise teacher will be slow to jump to conclusions. If you suspect a serious problem, involve your administration and resource personnel.

THE CHARACTERISTICS OF THE "SPECIAL CASE"

When you feel that perhaps you have a "special case" involving the normal child with excessive withdrawal patterns, it is important that you become aware of the frequency, the length, the breadth, and the depth of the wihtdrawal patterns. Ask yourself, "Are they really excessive? Are they increasing? Are they becoming a problem to me, the teacher, or to the child, or to the other children who are his peers?"

For example, Raymond is in the sixth grade and is the only child of successful professional parents. Their standards are high. At home Raymond is expected to follow a daily schedule of work and study. He is given little personal freedom. He is under constant, and often nagging, pressure from both parents to do better than they had done as children, and to take advantage of the opportunities that they never had.

He is in need of time to be alone with himself. His solution is to withdraw from the class to his private world. He looks out the window for minutes at a time and is unaware of anything that happens in the class.

This behavior pattern presented no problem for the first four grades because Raymond's intellectual capacity was such that he could keep up with the class. But by the fifth, and especially the sixth grade, the frequency and length of his withdrawing patterns became the direct cause of lower grades. These lower grades, of course, increased his home pressure, which in turn increased the duration and frequency of his withdrawing periods. Raymond was now a "special case." Why? Because:

- His behavior patterns involving withdrawal had become excessive.
- There was increase in the breadth of separation between his fantasies and the reality of the classroom.
- His withdrawal patterns were becoming a problem co Raymond himself, to the teacher, and to the class.

Like Raymond, any child who becomes a "special case" is no longer able to cope with himself or the society around him.

Whether the child returns to normal, remains a "special case," or even experiences excessive withdrawal, will be determined at least in some measure, by what you, his teacher, or some other equally potent parent figure can do to help him face reality in an acceptable way.

Call it what you will, hiding, retreating, isolating, fantasizing, or daydreaming, withdrawal is frequently confused with other types of defensive or protective mechanisms. There is a fine line between withdrawal as a behavior pattern and other defenses which may be interpreted as withdrawal, such as:

- Rebellion, where the child is refusing to participate because he is angry.
- Frustration, because others will not do as he wishes.
- Hostility, where he uses silence as a technique to control the teacher, principal, or class peers.
- Fantasizing, in which the child establishes his own unrealistic world of make-believe.

Defensive techniques, such as these, may often be misinterpreted as a withdrawal syndrome. Usually, only a specialist can diagnose and determine the extent of the problem and to what degree several defensive techniques may be involved or overlap.

However, by the time the child has developed into a "special case," the astute teacher, with careful observation, will have a concrete grasp of the behavior patterns of the child and of the general problem itself.

Well kept checklists and resumes of the child's history of behavior, will be of inestimable value as you reach your decision.

For the purpose of this chapter, withdrawal may be defined as: the behavior pattern adopted by a child who is hurt or is under severe enough pressure, either internal or external, to require him to retire into his own world, at least to the point where he usually is unable to function adequately in a school learning situation.

Once you suspect that a child is withdrawing, watch for the characteristics of the "special case."

GUIDELINES FOR PINPOINTING THE CHARACTERISTICS OF THE "SPECIAL CASE"

1 Be aware of changes in the withdrawal patterns of your class.

2. When you suspect that they are not normal, identify the child, or children refusing more and more to participate.

3. How does the child withdraw? There are many techniques:

   a) He may sit and refuse to talk or participate with the group.

b) He may stare out the window or doodle on the desk or paper.

c) He may sit in a corner, read a book, or do work that is unrelated to the class situation and routine.

d) He may wander aimlessly around the room or go outside and hide.

e) He may constantly perform some task an unnecessary number of times, such as going to the bathroom or sharpening his pencil.

f) He may refuse to leave the classroom at the proper break, or he may even go so far as to completely hide, especially during certain activities in which he feels threatened.

4. On the basis of your empirical evaluation, determine whether the length, depth, and frequency of withdrawal are increasing, and if perhaps the child is retreating further and further from the classroom situation.

5. In line with the above, is it becoming increasingly difficult for everyone, including yourself, to return the child to participation in the class or playground situation?

6. All of these characteristics are important, but do not of and by themselves indicate that the child has become a "special case."

DETERMINING TO WHAT EXTENT A CHILD IS BECOMING A "SPECIAL CASE"

Unlike "attention getting" patterns, those of withdrawal are often subtle and not easily delineated. What appears to be a withdrawal pattern may, in reality, be a completely isolated or a series of isolated behavior patterns.

The observant teacher recognizes that withdrawal is often related to, associated with, and strongly intertwined with other patterns that are protecting the child's psyche. On the other hand, she is alert to the symptoms, the frequency, the extent, and the possible causes of withdrawal patterns.

GUIDELINES IN DETERMINING WHETHER A "SPECIAL CASE" IS DEVELOPING

1. Does the child withdraw from only specific situations? For example, a child may refuse to participate in baseball, but will play

alone on the parallel bars. Another will participate in written class work, but will refuse to recite orally.

2. Does he withdraw from all participation in the classroom while engaging in playground activities, or does he withdraw from everything?

3. When does he withdraw? Is it at particular times of the day or week?

4. Does a specifically evident incident trigger his withdrawal? Watch for events such as:

    a) Eating.
    b) Going home at the end of the day.
    c) Vacations.
    d) Report cards.
    e) Parent-teacher conferences.

5. Does a definite individual trigger his withdrawal? For example, a peer who is present or absent, the appearance of the principal or of another authority figure.

6. Why is he withdrawing? From pressures, either external or internal? For instance:

    a) Increasing instability at home.
    b) A new school situation.
    c) Fears, such as those concerned with his own inability to succeed.

7. Is the withdrawal based upon a real or imaginary situation?

8. Is there a physical reason for withdrawal?

    a) Illness.
    b) Size.

9. Does withdrawal occur because of social maturity levels? Such as:

    a) Immature.
    b) Over-mature.

10. Is withdrawal connected with intellectual capacity? With achievement levels? The child who is too smart and who is not intellectually stimulated will withdraw. At the other end of the spectrum, the child who is unable to comprehend what is going on will withdraw to an environment where he is more comfortable.

To answer these questions, use the checklists you have developed for yourself from the examples given in the Appendix. Through them, you may move, step by step, to pinpoint the "special case," and to determine the extent of the problem.

HOW TO HANDLE THE CHILD WHO HAS BECOME A "SPECIAL CASE"

Automatically, as you employ your checklists to pinpoint the "special case," you will be instituting positive action toward helping the child. Four courses are open to you:

• You may accept the behavior patterns and allow the normal interpersonal relationships of the classroom and playground, in conjunction with the child's own corrective mechanism, to resolve the problem.

• You may tolerate the "special case" when it comes to withdrawal, especially if the child is creating no classroom or playground disruption, or if he is not physically hurting himself or his peers. The wisdom of such action is excellent if the child is basically withdrawn, but functions adequately enough to "get by" while maintaining a consistent level of productivity.

• You may be forced to refer the child to a specialist if all other efforts fail and there is a continuing deterioration in the child's behavior patterns. Referral should be done in consultation with the school's Pupil Personnel specialists and your administration.

Such referrals will happen very rarely in the elementary school. When they do, your checklists and resumes of your counseling will be of inestimable value. There will be specific written notations as to the time of withdrawal, when it was first noticed, the fluctuations of the patterns, disciplinary and counseling results, and the extent and speed with which the deterioration has occurred.

• Your own carefullly thought out and consistently followed counseling program to help the "special case" child will often alleviate his abnormal, withdrawing patterns. Use your checklists to determine progress and to record the effectiveness of your techniques.

GUIDELINES AS YOU COUNSEL THE CHILD WHO HAS BECOME A "SPECIAL CASE"

1. Determine through observation and talking with the child, from what he is trying to withdraw. From what is he running? From

whom is he attempting to escape? Are these persons, places, or things real or imaginary?

2. Help him to bring his fears and hurts, actual or fantasy, into the open. Through interpretation from you and verbalization on his part, you will enable him to analyze the reality of these fears and hurts. This may be done through talking with him individually or in a group. It may even be incorporated into sharing time or play activity. Here is an excellent opportunity for acting out situations in a form of socio-drama.

3. Chide him into determining what he really is afraid of, and whether it exists or is founded upon his imagination. Even if it does exist, has he distorted it out of all proportion? Is it a realistic fear?

4. Through supportive actions in a group, in a play situation, in special classroom attention, help him to cope with specific fear-producing situations. Aid him in trying to overcome them, or in learning to live with them if they cannot be overcome. Help him to recognize that it is acceptable to avoid situations he cannot possibly surmount. These vary according to the difficulty, the child's capacity, his age level, and countless other considerations.

5. Even though he is confronted by the harsh realities of life, and feels compelling needs to withdraw from them, you can relate his problems to similar ones that other students have, that you have, that his parents have, and that, in reality, everyone has to cope with.

Remember, a child has remarkable powers to solve or to resolve his problems. A few supportive words, such as the following, may help him immeasurably:

a) "Johnny, will you join us in this game?"
b) "Mary, I'm interested in how you feel about this subject."
c) "Tommy, I want you to succeed in spelling as well as in arithmetic."

Your assurance of love and encouragement will be most effective in helping a child face the fact that he is withdrawing.

6. Once the cause of withdrawal is faced and the problem is shared, most children evolve a more realistic and satisfactory defense pattern. They then return to their normal participation level.

The wise teacher will utilize peers and peer relationships to help draw the problem child back into the group. This is especially applicable on the playground. Expressed, increasing interest on your part will often mean decreasing withdrawal on the child's part.

7. The causes of withdrawal are almost unlimited in number. It is not always necessary to define them in order to resolve them. Sometimes just talking about the fact that the child has withdrawn, how much he is missing, and that others really want him, is sufficient to get him to open up and begin his own recovery program.

8. Every child is a human being with all the complexities implied. There is no specific nor perfect solution to the problem of withdrawal. What will work in one case will not necessarily succeed in another. What is effective with a certain child at one time may be of little value to him at another. Children are not created in one mold or one mood

Therefore, success is attained by trying the law of averages over and over again Eventually, this law will work with you. You will hit the winning combination, and then your little retreater will return to normal

9

Squirmers and
Little Shufflers

*Wriggles and giggles are normal
outlets for pent-up energies.*

Excessive body movements are to be expected from the elementary school child. Actually, a child's need for bodily movement is greater than that of an adult. He has less control of his physical movement; his body is young and all parts must have constant exercise and use. Within each little boy or girl there is a continual drive to release excessive amounts of energy.

Therefore, the wise teacher is attuned to each child's needs for various amounts of squirming, shaking the school desk, wiggling movable parts of clothing and equipment, plus giggling, dropping books, stamping feet, shuffling papers, pencils, crayons, etc.

Short learning periods are best for squirmers and little shufflers. Such periods should include individual or group projects, small group activities, classroom play, rest, and recess periods. When the length of time devoted to any specific learning or rest situation lengthens without interruptions and breaks, the amount of squirming and shuffling tends to increase in frequency and intensity. There is a marked positive relationship between the length of time of uninterrupted mental concentration and the increase in amount of bodily movements.

Like attention getting and withdrawal, bodily movement patterns are developed by every child. Through them he is able to accomplish certain goals:

1. He releases excess energy.

2. He relieves anxieties that have accumulated during periods of concentration.

3. He is giving needed exercise to muscle structure that—especially during growing periods—requires a tremendous amount of use.

4. He may be in need of a "change of pace" in order to re-attack the problem at hand.

Like the "coffee break" or "taking ten," excessive bodily movements help to tide a child over until an authorized class "break."

5. Frequently, excessive body movement may indicate a temporary physical imbalance.

A child may be running a fever, be hungry, or uncomfortable in a hot room. He may be coming down with a cold, chicken pox, or an upset stomach. He may even have an urgent need to use the bathroom more often than usual.

Perhaps he is experiencing a temporary trauma, such as:

- A skinned knee.
- An unresolved dispute with a peer, either in class or on the playground.
- A worry about pressing family problems.
- A loss of a sweater or a tearing of an article of clothing.

Bodily movements are a normal release of tension from such physical causes.

6. Certain days of the year, especially pre- and post-holiday periods, produce an atmosphere conducive to wiggling from anticipation or attempting to settle down.

Excessive body movements may take the form of wandering about the classroom or the school premises. The child may constantly do unnecessary chores such as:

- Sharpening and resharpening pencils.
- Restraightening or disorganizing books, chairs, and bulletin board materials.
- Making trips to the rest room, the cloak room, the office, or neighboring buildings.

When squirming becomes excessive, it always indicates that something is wrong. The cause may be as simple as a poor seating arrangement, weariness that comes at the end of a long hot day, or it may be as complicated as a hearing or vision problem.

Acute cases of excessive bodily movements may even indicate neurological impairment, or various forms of neuroses or psychoses.

In addition to being a problem by itself, excessive bodily movements may be one of the symptoms of a "special case" in almost any of the problem areas covered in this book.

GUIDELINES TO CONTROL EXCESSIVE BODILY MOVEMENT IN THE NORMAL CHILD

1. Realize that every one of us has to squirm if we haven't had a recent opportunity to stretch our muscles.

2. Schedule frequent changes of pace in presenting required classroom material. Allow for adequate stretching to meet individual needs.

For instance, Charles is intelligent, nervous, and constantly needs to please his teacher. His attention span is short; however, his ability to produce work is high. By excessive bodily movements he signals completion of an assignment.

His teacher, Miss H., with a minimal amount of available time and energy for Charles' problems, tries discipline. She places him in a corner seat saying, "Now Charlie, please sit quietly. Otherwise, you can't return to your regular seat."

This technique fails for two reasons:

   a) Charles physically can't sit still.
   b) His actions and personality are such that he can get the class to side with him. They watch his antics, instead of completing their assignments.

Miss H., recognizing her error, solves the problem through techniques of giving Charles extra work. She still maintains her discipline, but assigns the boy a series of future class reports. To dissipate additional bodily movement in an acceptable manner she also calls upon him to carry messages and equipment to other rooms and to the office.

3. Accept bodily movements as normal and tolerate them unless they are creating a disruptive force, whether to the learning patterns of a child or those of his peers.

4. Change the child's seat frequently with a verbalization, "Perhaps, Charles, you won't squirm so much over here."

Children respond well to such contact, plus a pat on the shoulder. It may enable them to stabilize themselves, or to express verbally the reasons for squirming. Usually, your reassurance will be felt and there will be attempts to control the bodily movements.

5. If the whole class is involved, try physical activity for everyone. Exercising by the individual seat is a good technique for releasing excess energy.

Your goal is not to fight each child's need for moving about. Help him meet this need as soon as possible and in the most acceptable way, insofar as the class, the student, and yourself are concerned.

6. When class squirming increases, organize specific playground activity. A hike or a fast game, where everyone must exert an excessive amount of physical energy, will often be effective.

7. Excessive body movements may indicate that you are not communicating adequately with your students. Increase communication by personalization.

You might say, "Jimmy, this next question is just for you," instead of "Jimmy, you're making too much noise thumping on the desk."

8. Inspect the physical facilities. Do they contribute to excessive movement by an individual or a group? Are certain seats too uncomfortable? Are the students too close to each other? Is the weather a factor? Is there too much noise or activity outside the classroom? Is the interruption rate too distracting? Can you control or in any way modify such facilities, or must you and your class learn to cope with them?

9. Flexibility in carrying out your work plan will be a key factor in curtailing excessive movements by an individual or by the entire class. Too big a dose of one specific activity may well create a problem.

10. Some forms of squirming and shuffling, wiggling and giggling, especially if they are premeditated or become a release of hostile feeling, may best be handled through positive action. Immediate and strong discipline is effective to control such a problem.

However, if excessive body movements originate from physical or emotional, unfulfilled needs, discipline will accomplish little. In fact, it may increase the severity of the problem.

EVALUATING THE COURSES OF ACTION

• As long as the child uses a large number of techniques, turning to specific ones only periodically and as a response to a real stimulus, the excessive bodily movement pattern may be regarded as normal.

• It is difficult to really determine whether a child's actions are

normal or whether he is becoming a "special case," for the following
three reasons:

    a) A large number of bodily movement patterns are used by
        most children.

    b) No one is able to gauge the extent to which it is sometimes
        necessary for a child to move.

    c) His need to move may vary from situation to situation.

• Use your checklists. Do you really have a child who is becoming a "special case" and is his problem one of "excessive bodily
movements?" Attempt to establish the causal factors in each specific
case.

• Don't categorize a boy or girl, even when giving him the
"special case" label Try to establish the cause or causes producing
the symptom.

• Your checklist will aid you in determining whether the class
in general is involved in a pattern of excessive bodily movements.
Is the problem increasing in frequency, intensity, and extent?

• Are you, in reality, facing one or more other problems? These
might be:

    a) Class rebellion.

    b) Overworked students.

    c) An inadequately oriented school or study program.

    d) An underprivileged or overprivileged group of students.

    e) Other problems discussed in this book, in which bodily
        movements may be present.

• Your checklists may be maintained by a teacher's aid or assistant. These records will help to determine quickly whether the class
as a whole is more than normally involved in bodily movements,
or whether a problem is centered around one or two individuals.

THE CHARACTERISTICS OF THE "SPECIAL CASE"

When you feel relatively certain that one or more of your students
have a problem of excessive body movement, watch for the characteristics of the "special case":

    1. Are one or two specific patterns consistently reappearing?

    2. Are these patterns disruptive to the individual and the class?

    3. Is the disruption increasing in frequency?

4. Does it extend over a greater length of time at each occurrence?

5. Are the excessive movement patterns more and more difficult to control? By the child? By the class dynamics? By you, the teacher?

For example, Ann C. was born with some brain and neurological damage. Her cerebral cortex functioned adequately so that she learned well. She did have difficulty with her musculature control. Her behavior patterns basically created no problem in the classroom situation until she entered fourth grade.

Then Miss Edith R., Ann's teacher, reported her anxieties concerning the child's increasing tendencies toward annoying excessive body movements. Ann constantly dropped books, papers, pencils. There was endless rearranging of clothing; the girl scratched, shuffled her feet, and doodled over the margins of her papers.

Medical evaluation determined that there had been a progressive, but slight, neurological deterioration involving muscular coordination. Prognosis was that this deterioration would continue.

The etiological cause of the "special case" happened to be neurological, it could just as well have been psychological. Very understandably, Ann's earlier teachers had regarded her as a "special case" emotionally.

With excessive bodily movements, a teacher will find it difficult to pinpoint whether the causal factors may be emotional, organic, or even a combination of both. Such determination—as in Ann's case—usually requires an extensive time lag, and the evaluation of several specialists.

However, Ann's problem was such that each of her teachers had to adjust to, and be able to accept the child as she was, at least until other arrangements—such as special class, home study, or some type of institutional day care—became practical for her.

Some of the techniques used to help Ann accept, and learn to cope with her problem, involved such specific counseling as:

a) Limiting the number of articles on her desk.

b) Encouraging her to wear clothing and adopt hair styles that required a minimum amount of care and rearranging.

c) Suggesting she use large pencils and large combs, rather than small ones.

    d) Scheduling her early arrival in class, in order to cause a minimal amount of confusion.

    e) Fostering class acceptance and toleration of Ann's problem and excessive movements.

Special arrangements were made about her written and blackboard work, oral recitations and playground activities, all of which she could participate in, but with severe limitations.

Similar techniques may be adapted to almost any "special case" involving excessive bodily movements. This is true whether the cause is physical, mental, or emotional. It is also true whether or not the cause has been established or delineated.

In observing the characteristics of bodily movement patterns, recognize that they may have been acquired in attempts to imitate the actions of a parent or a well-liked peer. Usually, calling attention to the fact that such actions annoy others, and therefore cannot be tolerated at school, is sufficient to correct them.

Movements, whether squirming or shuffling, picking at the body, playing with the hair, grinding things together, or pulling things apart, are indicators of a potential "special case." However, of and by themselves alone, they do not necessarily indicate a "special case."

DETERMINING TO WHAT EXTENT
A CHILD IS BECOMING A "SPECIAL CASE"

Excessive bodily movement patterns can become one of the most disruptive forces in the learning situation.

As additional individuals become involved in more and more unacceptable movement patterns, the classroom control may be taken away from you, the teacher. One child, several of your pupils, or even the entire class may usurp your power.

Therefore it is well to be on the alert for any excessive increase in the noise level, or the distraction level, of the class. Pinpoint whether or not these are caused by bodily movements.

GUIDELINES IN DETERMINING WHETHER
A "SPECIAL CASE" IS DEVELOPING

1. Observe who is involved. One? More than one? Is it always the same individual or group?

2. Determine the frequency and duration of the movements, use your checklists.

3. What specific bodily movements are involved?

4. Analyze the time of occurrence for both the peak and minimal amounts of movement. For instance, is the occurrence related to subject matter, recesses, specific times of the year, etc.?

5. Is there a discernible pattern? Is there a rapid increase, a steady increase, a fluctuating increase? Or, is there a decrease?

6. Is the pattern one of "follow the leader" or purely individual?

7. Is hostility or rebellion, against the school situation or the teacher, involved. This may be evidenced by the manner in which the students shuffle their feet, cough, or shoot paper wads.

8. Is it becoming more difficult to regain control of the students' interest after such interest has been disrupted by bodily movements?

9. When excessive disturbances cannot be controlled, do these get any results:

   a) Variation of teaching procedures.

   b) Fostering increased interest and attention through special rewards or punishments.

   c) Accelerating or decelerating the amount of work required from specific individuals.

If these or similar techniques fail, it is highly probable that you have one or more "special cases." Use your checklists to determine:

1. Who is your "special case?"

2. How severe is the behavior pattern of this case?

3. Is the behavior pattern increasing, decreasing, or chronic?

4. What triggers the bodily movement? Is there an apparent cause?

5. Does your empirical evaluation of this "special case" lead you to believe that you have:

   a) An ordinary disciplinary problem?

   b) An emotional problem that will require specific counseling?

   c) An organic problem that requires your special handling?

HOW TO HANDLE THE CHILD WHO HAS BECOME A "SPECIAL CASE"

By the time you have determined you have a "special case," you will have exhausted all your normal "bag of tricks" and the disciplinary techniques that should be successful in class control. Therefore, you will be aware that these stand-bys are relatively ineffective. Here are your guidelines:

- Isolate the problem child. Thus, you foster class learning, with a minimum amount of distraction.

Such isolation can be accomplished through:

   a) Seating arrangements, such as surrounding the child with peers who will not be affected, physically hurt, or upset by the bodily movements.

   b) Settling the child in a space where he cannot be readily seen, touched, or annoyed.

   c) Limiting his verbal, blackboard, or written participation.

   d) Unobtrusively eliminating articles that aggravate movement problems such as excess pencils, chalk, or paper.

   e) Prescribing specific assignments that help the child, such as assignments he understands but are not known to his peers.

   f) Special assignments, activities, evaluations when consistent with the school's requirements.

- Confine his learning periods and his class participation to those times of day when:

   a) Excessive body movements are at a minimum.

   b) He is emotionally prepared.

   c) He is physically more in control of himself.

- Through experimentation, determine what physical and mental activities, either in the classroom or on the playground, will dissipate his excess energy and leave him most amenable to the learning situation.

- Counsel with him individually. If several students have the same problem, counsel the group. Talk about:

   a) The problem itself.

   b) The effects of such movements upon personal well being as learning.

   c) The effects of excessive body movements upon the class.

   d) Acceptable ways to control unacceptable movement patterns.

As an example, the child who has to go to the bathroom continuously, because of nervous tension, can be reminded to go to the rest room at the beginning and end of each recess period. Under normal conditions, he would forget. Then, within a few minutes after the start of class, he would start to squirm. He may very well be innocently unaware of the need which causes his squirming.

- Set up specific playground activity that will conform to the child's physical or emotional need—we do not mean necessarily oriented around that child, but utilizing him in a group situation where he is able to drain off much of the energy involved in excessive movements. In addition, you will be giving the child opportunity to:

    a) Succeed in the group.

    b) Strengthen his own psyche.

    c) Conform to acceptable behaviour patterns.

• Provide outlets for the child's excessive movement needs through assigning extra tasks that involve coordinated movement, such as drawing, scissor-cutting, pasting, straightening shelves, taking down or setting up display boards. When giving such assignments, verbalize the reasons for assigning them.

For example, you may say, "Timothy, you need to move around a little. Set up these pictures on the display board. Carolyn will you help so that they are straight?" Or, "Johnny, we'll have to stop scuffling our feet. Take this jar over to the custodian's office and get us some more paste."

• When the child is an under-achiever, or an over-achiever, you may assign special projects involving manual skills or the collecting of various items in different areas. Thus, you will provide a learning situation that involves extensive accomplishment, as well as a release of excess energy. In addition, you may gain a moment for individual verbal counseling.

• A pat on the back, and an accompanying supportive verbalization, is an effective counseling technique. When done frequently, these positive acts tend to smooth out the child's excessive movements. This is especially true if there are indications that you are aware of how hard he is trying to conform to the desired patterns.

• Never lose the opportunity to give praise and implied approval. In determining the degree of success you achieve, what you say is not nearly as crucial as the way you say it.

10

Tears and Little Fears

Sensitivity and anxiety can work for or against us. Both are tools of creativity.

Children's emotions are close to the surface. An adult in most instances is adept at covering up his hurt and anxiety. A child finds it difficult to do so; he is so honest.

Because of this inability to hide his feelings, or to protect himself, a child frequently becomes defenseless. He is often carried away in the emotional torrent that is triggered by even a minor hurt or fear.

The wise teacher will expect tears and little fears as normal in helping the elementary child to mature.

Frequently, the more creative the child, the higher the level of sensitivity and anxiety. Both are tools of creativity. The anxious person strives to learn. He does what is expected of him and finds acceptable outlets for his needs.

Without anxiety, the human being becomes a vegetable. With anxiety, properly developed and used, he accomplishes the great goals of life. Improperly directed, anxiety may become a drive behind the great catastrophes, tragedies, and destructive forces of life.

The sensitive child is like a blank slate, and can be easily written upon, for good and for bad. This sensitive child can appreciate, understand, and accept almost anything; or he can be hurt to the point where he reacts negatively to almost all types of interpersonal relationships.

Sensitivity is like a two-edged sword. It can be used for or against the person who possesses it. Therefore, the elementary school teacher holds a key that may help every child with tears and little fears.

This help may be given through direct and indirect supportive counseling. Each child needs to achieve three goals:

1. To control and guide his feelings regarding himself and what he wants from life.

2. To utilize his anxiety and sensitivity in developing mature relationships with the world about him—his peers superiors, and inferiors.

3. To develop his abilities to live with, work with, and accept the feelings and needs of others.

Behavior patterns involving tears and fears are developed by every child as a defense and protection against the great unknown and unfathomable world about him.

Through these patterns he is able to accomplish certain objectives:

• He evades facing the reality of the moment.

• He is able to evoke a certain amount of sympathy and personal attention.

As an example, the crying child on the first day of kindergarten is doing his best to force his mother, the teacher, and all others he may encounter, to take him out of a new and threatening environment. He is struggling to get attention, and through it, to return home to security.

• He vents his feelings of resentment and hostility at being controlled and forced to conform.

• With each success, he reinforces a pattern that enables him to run from reality.

This is the reason that one of the best techniques in counseling such a child is to give a pat on the back, with the warm but firm matter of fact statement, "I understand how you feel, Joey, but we're going to have to go to school. You know, whether we like it or not, we have to grow up."

• He doesn't want to share his teacher, his mother, or other close emotional relationships with his peers. Tears help him avoid this sharing.

He gains release of tensions and related feelings. Even the child who is crying silently in the corner achieves this goal.

In every instance, the teacher has to judge, through her own feelings, whether to leave the child alone to cry himself out, whether to give him active support, or whether to take some other positive action.

- He achieves an opportunity to act out personal frustrations.

Children mature at many different rates. If unprepared to recite or to write, the over-sensitive child may protect himself through tears.

Tears and fears have value to each of us. Unfortunately, they are not always the best defense mechanism. An increase in their use is one of the earliest signs given a teacher that a child is not adjusting adequately to the school and playground situations.

GUIDELINES TO CONTROL TEARS AND LITTLE FEARS IN THE NORMAL CHILD

1. Accept the fact that you will have at least a few problem children in every class.

Always remember that only so much pressure can be applied to any particular child, or even to an entire class, at any particular time. If the pressure is too great, the fears and tears may become, at least temporarily, uncontrollable. Be aware of increasing pressures. Attempt to decrease and dissipate them.

2. To strengthen the crying child as well as his peers, use techniques such as the following:

   a) Allow him time to himself, and excuse him from performing until he has regained his composure.

   b) Change the pace, such as from a spelling assignment to a sharing time.

   c) Remove the child from the environment completely, possibly by sending him on an errand.

   d) Shift from studying to crafts, games, or drills. The object is to remove the child, or children, from the immediate pressures of a specific environment.

3. Be attuned to the fact that the tears may come from definite physical or emotional hurts suffered in the classroom, on the playground, on the way to school, or at home.

A word from you may enable the child to reveal whether the hurt is real or imagined, significant or immaterial. You will then gain insight in planning positive action to support him.

4. Observe the group dynamics. Will a change in the environment be helpful? Currently, is the child placed in a position so that he is:

   a) Attempting to achieve in a group from which too much is expected?

b) Picked on, or made fun of?

c) Out of place mentally, physically, or emotionally,?

It is important to remember that from a psychological point of view, even the slightest rearrangement changes an environment. As an example, the absence of one pupil from a class of thirty changes the environment. The effect on various members, as well as on the entire class, may be as great as a physical movement of the class from one room to the playground.

5. Don't fight a child's need to cry. Accept this need and endeavor to understand and support it. The possibilities are innumerable:

a) He may be suffering from an actual physical or mental hurt.

b) His crying, especially many types of whimpering, may be a strong indicator that he is physically ill. He may be coming down with the mumps, be suffering from undernourishment, or from an organic anomaly that keeps him always on the borderline between sickness and good health.

c) He is using crying as a defense to protect his psyche. He resorts to crying at any real or imagined invasion of what he considers his rights and privileges.

d) His crying is a technique of controlling authority figures or peer groups.

6. Determine what you and perhaps others can do to help him achieve his goals. You can:

a) Administer or supervise positive discipline in constructive and consistent patterns.

b) Give him a firm basis on which to build his own patterns of self-discipline.

c) Assist him in establishing more mature patterns of coping with his relationships to himself and others.

7. Adopt reward-censure techniques which do not foster tears and fears. Scolding, threatening, nagging, and making promises you cannot keep, will increase the child's insecurity and his inability to face reality.

8. Any physical bodily punishment is basically an admission of defeat. It cannot help a sensitive child. In many school districts, it is completely forbidden. Its effect is somewhat similar to electric or drug shock treatment. There may be a place for it, but only under very careful consideration and in line with the school district's overall policy for such action.

9. Oftentimes, parental attitudes will be responsible for the excessive fears a student shows toward teachers, administration, and the entire control pattern of the school situation. This is especially true if the parents, when they were children, had poor relationships with school authorities.

Continuously employ verbal reinforcement concerning the good things about school. Thus, you will help the child cope with the fears instilled at home.

It is extremely difficult to ascertain when a child is becoming a "special case" of tears and fears. This is particularly true if the symptom of tears is based on nebulous fears. As with an adult, nebulous fears fluctuate. They are difficult to pinpoint and to delineate even with professional help.

Use your checklists. Attempt, whenever possible, to discover causal factors in each specific case.

EVALUATING THE COURSES OF ACTION

• When you, the teacher, can determine that a child cries for a specific and logical reason, or that his fears are based upon realistic situations, you may regard his crying and anxiety as relatively normal.

• The grade and maturity levels of the child are major considerations in determining what may be a normal amount of crying in a specific situation. A sixth grade child may have just as many anxieties as a child in kindergarten. However, the well adjusted sixth grader's emotional defenses are more developed. He will not express his fears in the same way; that is, by an abnormal amount of crying.

A fifth grader who is periodically bursting into tears may be regarded as a "special case," while the first grader exhibiting the same symptoms may be considered relatively normal. He may need more than the normal amount of support and counseling, but he is still not a "special case."

• Your empirical opinion, backed by written records, will aid you in pinpointing the "special case."

• Fears and crying are contagious. Use your checklists to determine whether the class in general is involved in tears or whether you have one or two "special cases."

• These lists will aid you in determining whether the problem is increasing, decreasing, fluctuating, or remaining static.

• Likewise, these notations will be invaluable in pinpointing whether the problem is really fears and tears. It may in reality, be another or a combination of other psychological problems.

• Children are very susceptible to and attuned to the moods of those around them. They tend to be sympathetic and easily identify with others. An upset home, a distraught teacher, a community or school in turmoil, or anxious fellow students will invariably increase the anxiety level and the flow of tears in the average elementary school child.

This is normal and must be taken into account in attempting to ascertain who is becoming a "special case."

THE CHARACTERISTICS OF THE "SPECIAL CASE"

Actually, it is very easy to recognize the "special case" of tears and little fears. In a word, watch for "moreness."

1. Does the child cry more and more without apparent reason?
2. Do you find it more and more difficult to console him?
3. Is an increasing amount of effort on the part of the class, the child himself, or the teacher, needed to change his behavior pattern of fear and unhappiness to one of class or playground participation?
4. As a teacher you can tolerate only so much crying and associated disruptions. Tantrums, hollering, whimpering, and quiet weeping in a corner are distractions that may cause you to lose control of your class. At a minimum, they seriously hamper the learning situation.

For your own mental health, and the good of the class, take an immediate and positive approach to resolve the "special case."

Edward L., in the third grade, is a good example. He is small, relatively anemic, and very fearful. He was born with a heart murmur, and has been sick much of his childhood. A sympathetic family, fearful about his health, has catered to his every whim. A few tears would invariably get him attention, love of sorts, and gratification of his immediate need.

"I'm afraid Eddy is not physically able to do this," was the coddling remark most frequently heard from his mother and big sister. Fears and tears conditioned his every attempt to cope with his environment. In fact, Edward has always been a "special case'

From his physician's point of view, Edward could now participate in any activity of his third grade. However, he had been so conditioned to his privileged illness that he would not accept a normal role. Unless something positive is done to help Edward overcome his fears, he will always remain a "special case."

But what can a teacher working alone in a classroom do to help Edward, or another like him? There are many specific counseling techniques, individually as well as in a group situation, that any teacher may use. Some of these techniques are to:

a) Help the child accept the reality that he is no longer sick. This statement must be stressed with warmth and love, and in many ways. The concept of his good health must be stressed again and again.

b) Set up play or classroom situations involving physical activity. Repetitive consistent success, even in small doses, is important. Specifically point out successes by the child.

c) Help the family to approach in a realistic manner the child's need to face the situation that he or she is no longer sick.

d) Let the child know directly, as well as indirectly, that you will not allow his illness to be used as a weapon to maneuver you or the class.

e) Employ incentives that will work in a "special case" such as Edward's. Discipline in its ordinary sense will probably not be effective. Consistency in your required standards of performance will.

f) Avoid such phrases as "Oh, you're not sick!" These belittle the child and increase his fears. Choose other phrases, such as, "See, you did that just as well as anybody in class. You're much stronger than you realize, especially when you really try." It is not always what you say, but how you say it that determines your success in counseling.

Consistency of your requirements, plus impersonal enforcement of them is essential in helping such a "special case." Most "special cases," such as Edward can be returned to normal with such a positive approach. Begin as soon as you suspect the need for action. Carry your program forward with warmth and understanding.

5. The axiom, "the wheel that screeches gets the most grease," applies to the child who creates a disturbance. He gets attention, but others may need your help too.

From the mental health outlook, the insecure boy or girl who cries silently and inwardly all alone, may well have a more severe problem than that of his screaming peer. The inability to release even a minimal amount of his feelings is a characteristic of many a "special case" of tears and little fears.

6. Carefully consider the child who silently cries with no obvious reason. Other behavior patterns may be involved in his actions. These may be:

- Withdrawal.
- Excessive attention getting.
- Excessive dependence.
- Other problems treated in these chapters.
- A combination of other problems.

7. In most "special cases," tears, whether big or little, are indicative of fears and hurts. Real or imagined, such fears have a solid basis as far as the child is concerned.

8. Fear is a primary emotion. Never forget that when:

a) Well based and realistic, fear is important for survival. Properly used, even by a small child, it is probably the most important protective device we have. The fear syndrome activates the human being to be prepared to run, to freeze, or to fight.

b) Unsupported, fears are a source of many emotional problems.

c) Fears, especially nebulous ones, may be warning signals of a potential "special case." Use your checklists to record them.

The prudent teacher will be constantly on the alert to forestall, and attempt to discover, the underlying causes of tears and little fears. When an individual becomes so fearful that he cannot function, professional help is urgent.

DETERMINING TO WHAT EXTENT
A CHILD IS BECOMING A "SPECIAL CASE"

In addition to tears, a child will manifest many other indications of fear. These include such physical symptoms as shaking, excessive perspiring, inability to talk coherently, cold hands and feet, hiding, running away, or becoming relatively immobile. Since many of these characteristics may also be symptoms of acute physical or mental illness as well as fear, it is important that some form of positive action be taken.

The old nursery rhyme says:

> "Tommy's tears and Mary's fears
> Will make them old before their years."[1]

In the same vein, if the tears and fears come from an acute physical or mental illness, you may have a situation that requires an immediate decision. Acute physical illness is not a respecter of time or place. If there is any question in your mind, the child should be given a medical examination. Utilize your chain of command immediately. Once physical illness is established or ruled out, you can pursue a course by which the extent and disposition of the problem can be determined.

GUIDELINES IN DETERMINING WHETHER YOU HAVE A "SPECIAL CASE"

1. As opposed to many other behavior patterns, that of tears and little fears requires relatively rapid action on your part as a teacher and a counselor.

2. Determine whether the entire class is involved. Is the pattern of tears and fears normal? Is it temporary?

3. Search for specific reasons for tears and fears. When these cannot be pinpointed, start the checklists that you have constructed on each child involved.

4. Immediately attempt to confirm or rule out any possible physical illness.

5. The alert teacher, even more than the parent, is often in a position to help the child face reality and learn to handle his tears and fears in a socially acceptable manner.

6. Watch for the child who is so emotionally upset that his crying is relatively continuous. If he exhibits many physical symptoms of acute fear and if he is unable to function in the learning situation, there is a strong possibility that he is in immediate need of professional psychological help. Involve your special services department. Should referral become a part of the picture, your checklists and your chronological evaluation of the behavior patterns will be of inestimable value.

Donna was an only child who basically had everything done for her. From the first day in kindergarten, she displayed evidence of

---

[1] Burton Stevenson, *Home Book of Proverbs*, p. 788.

fear—fear of the teacher, of her peers, and of the entire school atmosphere. She cried daily, wanting to go home. Unfortunately, the mother refused to support Miss S., Donna's kindergarten teacher. The girl's mother insisted that Donna be allowed to return home whenever she was upset. In time, the principal and Miss S. were successful in persuading Donna's mother to keep the child in school. Then Donna developed the technique of becoming nauseated. She found that vomiting could get her home immediately, in spite of her teacher's program to keep her in the classroom.

The family physician's assistance was sought. He found nothing organically wrong and suggested that Donna remain in school regardless of the nausea.

Miss S. recognized that she had a "special case" in Donna, and she:

a) Kept accurate records of Donna's progress.

b) Gave her support in every way possible.

c) Talked with the child frequently.

In addition, she observed that Donna was utterly unable to protect herself either in the classroom or on the playground. She was the brunt of hostility, constantly being pinched, hit, and annoyed. Her defense, now that she was no longer allowed to go home, became a silent, stifled crying. She sought constant refuge at the skirts of Miss S.

The many counseling techniques perfected by Miss S. in a decade of teaching now failed her. The child's symptoms of fears deepened. Physically, Donna began to break out in a rash. Having evaluated Miss S.'s records, and aware of the deteriorating situation, the family physician recommended that Donna be removed from the school environment, and be given intensive psychological counseling. This proved effective and the child was successfully returned to school within four months.

7. Your checklists, as in the case of Miss S., can be invaluable in helping your chain of command determine the advisability of referral for the "special case."

8. However, with the average "special case," there will be no need to refer. You, the teacher, will be in the most advantageous position to help the child:

a) Cope with his fears.

b) Accept the reality of school.

c) Develop defense techniques that serve him better than crying.

GUIDELINES AS YOU COUNSEL THE CHILD WHO HAS BECOME A "SPECIAL CASE"

With the child who is persistently and constantly tearful and fearful, there are many approaches and counseling techniques that you may employ to help him resolve his problems.

1. Whenever possible, aid him in verbalizing his fears. Talk about:

- What he is afraid of.
- Why he is afraid of it.
- Why he feels he has to cry.
- What his unacceptable behavior accomplishes.
- What he can do to cope with fear.

2. Help him to discover how others handle the same or similar problems.

This goal is often best accomplished in a group-sharing type of situation. Basically, this is a form of group therapy. It produces many of the same goals. Such group interpersonal relationship helps the child to desensitize his fears and live more realistically with his problems.

3. Through his intellect, assist him in recognizing the difference between his grounded and ungrounded fears. The basic differences are:

   a) Grounded fears are realistic and have to do with basic survival, such as:

   - The fear of being hit by a car when crossing the street.
   - The fear of being punished when doing something wrong.
   - The fear of being held up to ridicule, especially if this has been previously experienced.

   b) Ungrounded fears are excessive concern about relatively improbable events, or excessive fears about normal fear-provoking situations, such as:

   - Fear that an airplane will fall on the school; which might happen, but would be relatively improbable, and would be an event no one could control.
   - Fear of not growing any bigger, or being hit by a car while not even crossing the street.

• Fear that mother will die in the morning and leave.

4. In addition, help the child to develop appropriately mature reactions to normal fear-provoking stimuli. For example, a child may have three basic reactions to flying baseballs on the playground:

a) Appropriately mature reaction: He keeps a "weathered eye" open for flying baseballs, and he is aware that they may hit him. He is prepared to duck for safety.

b) Under-reaction (immature): He pays no heed to baseballs being thrown, and even wanders unconcernedly among these flying missiles.

c) Over-reaction (immature): He is constantly afraid of being hit by a baseball, even though there are no balls being thrown on the playground.

5. Counsel him to heed his fears. Explain that they are normal, protective devices. If over-used, they will not work for him when he needs them. If under-used, they will not protect him, and he may be severely injured.

6. Help him accept the fact that everyone has fears. Remind him that he must live and adjust to his society.

7. Aid him in understanding his fears. The unknown is usually the greatest source of ungrounded fears. We are afraid of being hurt. When we know what can and cannot hurt us, then we are more secure and are usually able to live with our fears.

8. Give adequate training in such procedures as fire drills, disaster drills, and simple first-aid techniques. Follow the methods used by your school system and explain these and other similar procedures again and again. Such explanations will often overcome excessive fears experienced by the "special case," and may prevent development of these fears by the normal child.

9. Fears often relate to the following and similar situations:

• Death.
• Accident.
• Desertion.
• Not being chosen or accepted.
• Illness.

Periodically, in any teaching situation, opportunities present themselves for explanations that will tend to decrease your student's specific fears regarding any catastrophe. Be aware of the need to use such occasions and make the most of them.

10. A supportive and success-inspiring atmosphere in the classroom will do much to return the "special case" of tears and little fears to normal. When it comes to rehabilitating the "special case" of excessive tearfulness and fearfulness, the approach, the mood, and the consistent attitude of the teacher and other authority figures will set the tenor of the environment in which the child can successfully resolve his problems.

11

Excessive Dependence and Little Hypochondriacs

A child must satisfy his needs. He can do so positively or negatively. Fostering ill health and excessive dependence is negative, and basically ineffective.

Maturing is a process of growing independence.

The newborn child is completely dependent upon someone for all his needs. Almost immediately, he begins, step by step, to break the ties of dependency. He learns relatively early to feed himself, thus attaining a degree of maturation.

Maturation occurs slowly, and probably is never attained completely. As the adage goes, "No man is an island unto himself."

The mature individual is aware of, and accepts the fact he is dependent upon others for the fulfillment of many of his needs. However, excessive dependence at any age is an emotionally unhealthy state.

Therefore, the astute teacher, as well as the wise parent, daily attempts to help each child protect himself, take care of himself, think for himself, act for himself, and in general, increase his independence.

In fact, it might be said that the focus of education is to help each individual increase his independence, thus becoming more proficient in meeting his needs. All of his growth in independence, of course, must be compatible with the needs, mores, and requirements of the society in which the individual lives.

In any normal elementary class, several cases of excessive dependence may exist. Note the child evidencing these patterns:

1. Asking his peers to do everything for him.
2. Inveigling his family into satisfying an excessive number of wishes and needs that he should be able to attain for himself.
3. Even succeeding in persuading you, his teacher, to coddle and pamper him.
4. Developing excessive dependence upon his natural proficiency in one specific area, such as:

   - On the playground.
   - In a specific subject.
   - In extracurricular activities, such as appearing in programs for the PTA.

5. Becoming dependent upon his ability to "mooch" materials, favors, and sympathy from everyone around him.
6. Making use of special talents or skills to fulfill his needs.

This excessive dependence may not be readily discernible because of his pleasing personality or his ability to feed the ego needs of others.

George G. arrived in high school with a background of average marks. In tenth grade, he failed miserably and dropped out during the first semester. His parents, professionally trained, were concerned and anxious because they had hoped George would go to college. He was brought to me for counseling.

George was, surprisingly, unable to read, write, or do arithmetic. Yet his report cards through elementary and junior high school indicated that he was only slightly below average.

I soon discovered that much of his problem centered around excessive dependency upon one skill; he was a superb draftsman and artist.

Early in elementary school, George found that he could please nearly everyone, and still not accomplish what was really required of him. He had maintained satisfactory marks through the simple process of doing extra projects in every subject. He used his ability to draw. As he pleased his teachers, they coddled him.

In spelling class, he drew charts with the words on them. He didn't learn the words, but the charts were displayed all over the school, and brought praise to George and his teachers. When history was being studied, he drew pictures of famous people and events.

These were shown at community functions, and again created recognition for George and he teacher. However, he learned nothing about history.

From a realistic point of view, we must accept the fact that George's skill won't take him through high school or college. He is a "special case" academically because he lives in a world of his own and is excessively dependent upon one ability. In all probability, this ability will enable him to be very successful in earning a living, as well as being liked by his fellow townsmen. However, his success will be in limited areas, largely because of his complete lack of education.

The excessively dependent child may use ill health, either real or imagined, to control authority, superiors, inferiors, and peers. He may feign sickness, aches, pains, major scratches, etc. This becomes an excellent means of obtaining self-love, a way to be babied, pampered, receive sympathy, privileges, or the fulfillment of other needs.

In fact, excessive dependence upon ill health or imagined ill health, may turn any child into a little hypochondriac.

A little hypochondriac who has become a "special case" is, for purposes of this chapter, classified as:

"One who has hypochondria—abnormal anxiety over one's health, often with imaginary illnesses." [1]

This is not the exact definition generally used in medical and psychiatric evaluations. The teacher working with this type of "special case" must be acutely aware that, like many other symptoms, discussed in this book, those that lead to a definite neurotic or psychotic label of a child can be specifically pinpointed only by a qualified medical or psychological specialist. Such a specific diagnosis is arrived at only after detailed testing and evaluating.

With the problems of excessive dependence and hypochondria, a number of techniques frequently are adopted by the "special case." He may:

- Utilize the excuse of illness after recovery from the illness.
- Imagine illness, where none exists.
- Imitate the symptoms of a peer's illness to gain sympathy or to satisfy his personal and sometimes very specific needs.
- Seek the sympathy and the pity of those around him.

---

[1] *Webster's New World Dictionary of the American Language* (New York: Popular Library, Pocket-size edition), 1958.

Unchecked tendencies to use illness or other overdependent be-havior patterns as a crutch, or a defense mechanism, tend to lead to extreme neurotic and psychotic patterns later in life.

Therefore, for the well-being of the child and the school situa-tion, it is important that every teacher be aware of what the normal and the abnormal syndromes may be in a child's dependent-independent relationships for each particular maturity level.

GUIDELINES TO CONTROL
EXCESSIVE DEPENDENCE AND UNREALISTIC
FEELINGS OF ILL HEALTH IN THE NORMAL CHILD

1. Never forget that a proper balance of dependence-inde-pendence is essential to the mental health of all of us.

2. When normal and healthy techniques fail a child in realizing this balance, he may regress to an earlier level, where he was more dependent and felt more secure.

3. Excessive dependence evidences itself in many ways. These are often so subtle, obscure, and unobtrusive that they are scarcely noticeable until the "special case" situation is completely upon you.

4. Through unrealistic feelings about, and use of, ill health, a child can learn to:

    a) Control this dependent-independent relationship to his ad-vantage.

    b) Avoid accepting normal responsibilities.

    c) Manipulate his peers in an infantile manner.

    d) Maneuver authority figures, such as parents, teachers, neigh-bors, etc.

5. Each teacher, like each parent, must guard against the perfectly natural tendency to be oversolicitous of the child who is well, physically, and over-protective of the one who is, or has been, ill or injured.

6. Each child's best interests are served by gradually pushing him away from the dependent security of the "nest." This pushing is done step by step from the day he enters kindergarten and until he leaves elementary school. In reality, the same process, only at a higher level, starts again in junior high and senior high school.

7. As you teach and counsel a child, the most important ingredi-ent in helping him become independent, is your empathy. When you understand how he feels, and you can accept his feelings and

yet avoid becoming emotionally involved, you will be effective in helping him grow.

8. In the same vein, it is unwise to smother his normal drives to attain independence.

9. Your sympathy is a very dangerous tool; it fosters dependency. With sympathy, you identify with the child, and want to protect him from the normal bruises and hurts of his environment. The maturing process requires that each child learn to cope with the reality of life's "hard knocks."

Your pity, often a part of sympathy, is a form of rejection. It induces the child to reinforce only feelings of self-pity that he may have. Self-pity deprives him of normal desires to be healthy and to grow up and to become independent. If smothering must occur, leave it to the parents. It is not for you, his teacher.

A child is very much like a rosebud; both need all the elements to grow. They must be in the right amount. If the gardener gives the plant too much or too little, the plant suffers, and so it is with a child. Love doesn't smother a plant or a child; it cultivates and provides the best environment available under the circumstances. Love doesn't push or control, it provides the opportunity for growth and the child carries on from there.

Unrealistic or unwarranted praise is also a subtle form of rejection, because it is easily recognizable as insincere. A child needs recognition for what he does, not praise for something that he, as well as his peers, will know that he did not accomplish.

10. Honest appreciation, expressed directly and indirectly, will help a child evaluate his own worth and seek his own independence.

11. Be tolerant of excessive dependence at certain short periods, whether or not you can pinpoint the causes. In times of acute stress, most of us need to turn to someone or something for security. Usually at that point we need to be overly dependent.

12. As and when excessive dependence appears to increase, whether individually or in large groups, recognize its presence. Verbally point out to your class, as well as to the individual child, that everyone needs to grow and become self-reliant. Stress how this may be done. Dependency needs may be directed toward many persons, places, and things. The degree and extent may consciously be decreased by your own personal awareness.

13. In your daily routines in class and on the playground, be alert to subtle pressures infringing on your time and energy. Are

these pressures the symptoms of developing excessive dependency on the part of the individuals or groups?

14. Too frequently, verbal or physical punishment may reinforce the child's techniques of fulfilling certain dependency needs in negative ways, such as:

  a) Receiving pleasure from pain.
  b) Interpreting punishment as love.
  c) Taking abuse from peers just to be accepted.

15. Each of us must find ways to inflate our ego. Fostering pupil over-dependence is certainly one way of satisfying a teacher's need to be important and indispensible. How often have you heard a lamenting teacher in a moment of self-pity whine, "Well, at least my students appreciate me."? The wise teacher fills his personal needs in a more acceptable manner.

EVALUATING THE COURSES OF ACTION

1. From the very first day of school, it is important to guard against allowing any child to use you as a haven of refuge. Orient all of your techniques toward helping each child face the realities of growing up. As he faces himself, he gains independence.

2. Close observation will enable you to determine whether a child is:

  a) Acting excessively dependent.
  b) Fluctuating or changing in his dependency needs.
  c) Attempting to become more mature and gain independence.

3. Your considered analysis, plus written records, will alert you to the individual indications of hypochondria:

  a) Over-concern about present, past, or possible illness.
  b) Reliance on illness to fulfill increasing dependency needs.
  c) Frequency and duration of real or imagined illness.

4. Your recorded observations will:

  a) Enable you to tolerate acute, but temporary and therefore normal, patterns.
  b) Alert you to the problems and needs of a "special case."
  c) Lay the foundation for any testing which may become necessary.
  d) Prepare for the possibilities of future professional referral.

5. Because of the hidden and subtle forces involved in relationships between ill health and excessive dependency, any indication that a "special case" is developing will entail rather expensive and time-consuming procedures:

   a) Administrative confirmation of your suspicions.
   b) Parental involvement in the problem.
   c) An overall medical examination and prognosis.
   d) Psychological testing and evaluation by the special services department of your school, or by a certified or licensed clinical psychologist.

The team involved in the testing will then determine the course of action. Whether immediate and effective help can be given this "special case" will depend initially upon you, your counseling when you recognize the problem, your records and evaluations kept with your checklists, and your prompt involvement of your administration with any referral necessary.

THE CHARACTERISTICS OF THE "SPECIAL CASE"

Once you suspect that a child is excessively dependent, or is becoming a little hypochondriac, ask yourself, "Is he really a 'special case,' and why do I think he is?" Use the following guidelines:

1. Is the entire class dependent?

For instance, it is highly possible that the previous teacher developed strong teacher-student dependency relationships with which you will have to cope.

Miss Helen T. had been an extremely successful kindergarten teacher for over twenty years. Each succeeding year, she became more upset and unhappy when she faced the reality that her class must leave her and go into the next grade. Frequently, she would confide to the other teachers, "My greatest joy is in having former students come back and tell me how much they missed and needed me."

Thus, she created problems for the first grade teacher, Mrs. R., who each year started with a class of overly-dependent students. Usually there were one or two "special cases." However, Mrs. R. was able to nurture the children's normal desire for independence.

"Miss Helens" appear in varying degrees in many school systems. Fortunately, most children can cope with this relationship and exert their normal and successful striving for independence. Too often though, it produces a few "special cases."

2. It is important, both to the well-being of the child and the health of the classroom situation, that you pinpoint at once the first indications of excessive dependence expressed in the form of hypochondria.

3. The symptoms of over-dependence may vary. They may be cloaked in many devious or straightforward actions and activities. One thing, however, stands out. There is an ever-increasing need on the part of the child for your time, your attention, your approval, your disapproval, and even your verbal or physical punishment.

4. Unchecked, the growth of excessive dependence can lead to an extremely maladjusted personality and grave unhappiness for the individual himself and others involved in his life.

5. Positive action must be taken to help the child who is too dependent, or who has unrealistic tendencies to hypochondria. This action may be taken by you, by others around the child, by the child himself, or by a combination of these individuals.' However, without meaningful help, a steady deterioration process may well place him in such a state that he may never adequately mature.

Surprisingly enough, the excessively dependent individual or the hypochondriac may become highly educated or trained. In spite of such abilities, he may still be unable to attain the self-reliance and independence necessary to establish his own family unit, or to assume a truly adult role of leadership in our society.

6. Force yourself to face the reality of the situation. You can be too understanding. Pinpoint the child who is developing into a "special case," design a set of checklists that fit your needs and use them. Be quick to enlist help from others involved with or in a position to help you with your "special case."

DETERMINING TO WHAT EXTENT
A CHILD IS BECOMING A "SPECIAL CASE"

It is perfectly normal for every child to be excessively dependent at certain times and in certain situations. This is always true when more than normal amounts of pressure are being applied at home, at school, or at play, by his peers, the child himself, or by authority figures.

In fact, you can anticipate that nearly every child will become a "special case" at least for a short lived crisis at sometime during the school year. This situation is normal, provided there is an almost immediate return to an acceptable independent-dependent relationship.

GUIDELINES IN DETERMINING WHETHER A "SPECIAL CASE" IS DEVELOPING

1. Is the excessive dependence, or reliance upon illness, noticeable only at specific times, and in a limited number of situations?

For example, does dependency increase at recess time when Mary is forced to compete physically? Is it most noticeable when the last bell has rung and one or more children exhibit behavior patterns that indicate they are afraid to face the realities of going home? Does it occur when David is forced to recite?

2. Has the child apparently developed techniques of using excessive dependence, or even illness itself, as a means of achieving goals, such as:

   a) Getting his way?

   b) Hiding?

   c) Maneuvering others?

   d) Satisfying personal drives?

3. It is becoming increasingly difficult to return the child to an acceptable level of independence?

4. Is there an obvious or a realistic reason for the extent of the problem? Is it:

   a) Physical?

   b) Intellectual?

   c) Emotional?

   d) Realistic or unrealistic?

5. "An ounce of prevention is better than a pound of cure."

If the symptoms of dependency are readily noticeable, and are steadily increasing, there is a strong possibility that a real problem is developing. Take action at once. Establish checklists that fit your needs. Early and consistent use of your lists will enable you to pinpoint the excessively dependent child, and assist you in determining what problems you, as well as the child, may be facing. In addition, the checklists will be helpful in relation to avenues open to the child in resolving the problem. They will give you a sense of direction that will enable you to cope more effectively with the problem on the playground, and in the classroom. You will have an available record of your progress as you help the child resolve his dependency needs in a more acceptable way.

HOW TO HANDLE THE CHILD
WHO HAS BECOME A "SPECIAL CASE"

Basically, there are only three courses of action open to you when it comes to a child displaying the symptoms of excessive dependence and/or hypochondria.

1. You may accept, or tolerate the situation, hoping that either the child will work it out for himself, or that the classroom dynamics will enable him to resolve his problems.

This is a poor course of action even for a short period, because in most instances, there is a need for a positive push in the right direction from some authority figure. The amount, the direction, and the extent of the push will vary, depending upon the individuals involved, your capacities, and what you feel your checklists indicate.

Every child lives in the immediate moment; from his point of view, he needs help right now, whether his problem is physical, mental, or emotional.

2. You may find it necessary to refer the child for professional help, either through your special services department, or to a private source. This, however, occurs rarely at the elementary level, and only when the situation has become intolerable to the class, the administration, and probably even to the parents.

3. You will generally find it possible to give a child all the help he needs in attaining a desired level of independence. In fact, it is a constant source of surprise and personal satisfaction to discover your ability at helping a child who apparently cannot be helped, as he succeeds in this maturation process.

GUIDELINES AS YOU COUNSEL THE CHILD
WHO HAS BECOME A "SPECIAL CASE"

Each "special case" is different. However, you can use the following guidelines to advantage:

• Foster independence in the entire classroom and playground situation. This can be accomplished both in an individual and a group situation, whereby your praise is given for independent thought and action.

- Don't be over-protective. Teach the value of trial and error. Experience is still the best teacher.
- Encourage decision-making. A poor decision, made by the child, whether successfully implemented or not, is better than your "pat" decision, or no decision at all. Such decision-making is essential in any favorable growth pattern. Establish a successful climate, and normal patterns of maturation evolve.
- A child's sense of independence is like his muscles. It must be exercised if it is not to atrophy.
- Similarly, a child's independence must be socially acceptable and compatible with his environment.
- By verbalization and by structuring and interpreting various areas of play, whether inside or outside the classroom, help the child to become aware of his dependency.

Use such phrases as, "Now, Johnny, you don't need my help to do that," or "Phyllis, does your head really hurt, or is this just a way to avoid having to read aloud?" or "Tommy, even if the other boys did walk off and leave you, don't cry and feel sorry for yourself. You can still walk home alone and enjoy it."

- As the child overcomes specific dependency symptoms, give your approval and support, both physically and verbally, with pats on the back and a word of encouragement. Step by step, force the child to stand alone.
- Maintain positive pressure to help each child grow in independence and ability to face the harsh realities of life. Continuous support and approval by you and his peer group will help him in attaining maturity.

A child, like an adult, needs a change of pace from pressure. Without it, any number of problems may result. We generally function better when doing the activities we like and do well. For instance, the child who may feel too sick to recite in class, may feel well enough to play not only one, but two innings of ball during recess.

- Play it by ear.

No child can be forced to achieve too much too soon. We become independent slowly. However, even in cases of extreme personal disability, in the area of dependency, you the teacher may be very effective in helping the overly-dependent child or little hypochondriac to assume his normal role in the school society.

12

Fantasyland:
World of Escape
for Little Daydreamers

*Daydreams—a well used release
when reality becomes too harsh.*

From time immemorial, mankind has fled from its problems via the road of daydreams. Our literature, our movies, even our modes of pleasure often take us by the hand as we escape into fantasyland.

For purposes of this chapter, the term *fantasy* is used interchangeably with "daydreaming," "make-believe," and "reverie." They refer to the normal and "special case" behavior patterns of escape that children in the elementary classroom often use.

The term *phantasy* is avoided because, from a psychological point of view, it refers to specific psychotic symptoms, such as *phantasy of being eaten, phantasy-life of ego,* and *masturbation phantasy.*

Much fantasy involves no conceivable current or potential value. However, fantasy, especially constructive or purposeful, is valuable to a fruitful life.

Any creativity—whether building a house or a philosophy of living—originates in someone's mind as a dream. For instance, we might still be walking down that backyard path to the "outhouse," or carrying water from the town pump, if some family hadn't fantasized about how comfortable it would be to have inside plumbing. Positive action on the part of someone then turned his reverie into a reality.

When confronted by a child displaying excessive fantasy, a

teacher must recognize that there is a fine line between daydreaming that may be eventually productive, and reverie that is solely a means of escaping a task at hand or an intolerable situation.

Fantasy is used by every child to satisfy certain needs:

- As a means of achieving a short physical and mental rest while resolving a tiring problem.
- As a way of momentarily escaping from the physical or mental pressures imposed by himself or others.
- As a method of organizing, or grouping, his thoughts or ideas for a future project.

  For example, Carl may tire of spelling and drift into fantasizing the possible line-up for a ball game later in the day.

  On the other hand, Betty may be preoccupied with free association of words related to her spelling lesson.

- As an avenue of escape from an intolerable situation, which may result from the physical environment, from hunger, lack of sleep, or even from boredom.
- As a projection into a happy situation. Steven hears the fire siren, looks out the window, and is off to become a hero. He imagines himself a fireman driving a shiny, big, red hook and ladder unit.

Such daydreaming is normal. It is often beneficial. However, it can create a problem when carried to extremes; therefore, the earlier a child is able to control the breadth, the width, and the extent of his daydreaming, the more rewarding his life will be. He must not allow daydreaming to become a basis for behavior which might tend toward the neurotic or psychotic.

GUIDELINES TO CONTROL DAYDREAMING PATTERNS IN THE NORMAL CHILD

1. Recognize that the child's mind and body are such that there is a constant need to get away, if only for a second. This is true in almost every type of activity. Such behavior is normal.

Johnny, who loves baseball, is playing center field. Momentarily, he drifts away on some unrelated avenue of thought. Forcefully, he returned to reality when hit by a ball he should have fielded. He may be unaware that he even drifted away. The reality of experience is a great teacher. When possible, use it in your direct counseling.

2. If fantasizing is from a momentary stimulus, it is difficult, and realistically of little value, to attempt to determine its cause.

3. To a greater or lesser extent, all children are governed by their flights of imagination. Often, they are physically incapable of concentrating upon a specific subject for more than a few seconds at a time. This is why it is important for the teacher to write assignments and salient points on the blackboard. Important concepts need to be verbalized more than once. A thorough speaker who wants his audience to remember what he says, tells them what he is going to say, then tells them about the subject, and finally summarizes what he has said. A well qualified teacher does the same. He knows his children, like any audience, will have moments of daydreaming during the learning period.

4. Foster the child's normal tendencies toward daydreaming, fantasizing, and reverie, provided that:

   a) These do not interfere with his ability to mature or learn.
   b) He does not develop socially unacceptable behavior patterns which would create problems within himself or those around him.

5. Help each child recognize that his daydreaming is important and has its function in his life.

   a) He must control it.
   b) He must utilize it.
   c) There is a preferred time and place for everything, even fantasy.

6. If the entire class, or a group of several children, is involved in excessive daydreaming, attempt to discover specific reasons, such as:

   a) Boredom, poor teaching situation, immediate physical environment, or other factors not conducive to long periods of concentration.
   b) Over-involvement or concern with another area of interest, at school, at home, or at play.
   c) Conscious or unconscious techniques used to get attention, control others, escape from a situation, satisfy specific needs, or attempt to fulfill vague desires.

7. Determine whether fear is involved, and find ways to desensitize it through activity as well as verbalization.

8. Insofar as the normal child is concerned, punishment may well increase the depth and extent of the fantasy. Adopt classroom and playground techniques of control which will help the child to:

  a) Differentiate between make-believe and reality.
  b) Accept the need of every individual to fantasize about a situation that cannot be tolerated.
  c) Identify and distinguish between sincerity and insincerity in his own actions and in the actions of others.
  d) Recognize and cope with socially desirable and acceptable needs to dissent, to conceal facts, and to actively lie about certain situations or facts.

For example, it is relatively well known that Mary's father is in prison. Part of the class may believe Mary's story, that her father is away on a business trip; but others having heard their parents discuss the imprisonment, may taunt Mary about her father's actual whereabouts.

Mary's story is not her own; it is her mother's fantasy, created to "save face" for their family. Mary, taunted to hysteria, forces the teacher's hand.

Miss B. recognizes Mary's need to conceal the facts and the reason for the lies. She very wisely does not discuss the taunting or even the fantasized story. Instead, she verbalizes for the entire class, the value of "minding your own business." She stresses the importance of concentrating on your own problems, rather than taking out your frustrations, anxiety, and hostility on others.

9. Analyze your own personal daydreaming and fantasy. The techniques you have perfected for yourself will give you a firm basis from which to work in helping your pupils. Perhaps you might:

  a) Put specific control on your amount of daydreaming.
  b) Allow a certain time and place for fantasizing to "run wild."
  c) Recognize when you are fantasizing, and whether you are helping or harming yourself, as well as others.
  d) Be aware of when you are using fantasy as a means of escape.
  e) Control fantasy to give it potential value. This is what

is actually done when the technique of "brain storming" is used in business problem solving sessions, or the technique of "free association" is used in mental health problem solving sessions.

f) Recognize fantasy in others.

EVALUATING THE COURSES OF ACTION

• When it comes to the child's behavior patterns that involve daydreaming, the positive approach is the most constructive.

• It is normal to be impatient with the pupil who daydreams. However, all children need to daydream and some need to daydream more than others. Unless there is a specific change in a child's normal pattern of fantasy, he may be regarded as making an acceptable adjustment to life.

• It is a truism that everyone needs time to create, to imagine, to recoup one's frayed defenses, and to successfully bathe one's self in the impossible.

• Your best test of whether a child is becoming a "special case" of daydreaming is two-pronged:

   a) Is there a marked differential between his previous and present learning curve? This will include intellectual, physical, social, and emotional growth.

   b) Is he becoming more and more out of touch with the realities of the classroom, the playground, and his fellow human beings?

• Use the checklists you design for evaluating this type of behavior problem. They will help you decide whether a child is normal or is becoming a "special case."

THE CHARACTERISTICS OF THE "SPECIAL CASE"

It is relatively easy to distinguish the child who lives a part of his time or most of his time in fantasyland. Watch for these characteristics of the "special case":

1. Pinpoint the child, or children, indulging more and more in fantasizing. "Moreness" is always a "red flag" warning of a possible "special case."

2. Be aware of any increase in the amount of time consumed

by the class, a group of boys and girls, or a specific child using daydreaming as a defense.

3. How does the child actively fantasize? The techniques he uses will give you clues as to his needs, and how he may be trying to fulfill them. Use these clues as starting points for your evaluation and in your counseling.

a) Does he want to monopolize time with wild imaginative stories?

b) Do his daydreams involve the use of classroom materials, such as clay or paper products?

c) Does he devise construction materials from playground discards or dirt?

d) Does he distort happenings at home?

e) Does he act out imagined situations?

f) Does he isolate himself and silently daydream?

4. Such fantasy may be considered as normal, unless the amount of time devoted to the actions increases, and the extent of the exaggerations digresses further and further from reality.

5. Watch for the signal flares that will indicate that a "special case" is developing. Ask yourself these questions:

a) Does it require more and more effort to return him to the realities of the immediate routines?

b) Can the child make this return without help?

c) Is effort required by peers, yourself (the teacher), or authority to help him return to reality?

d) Is his return only temporary?

6. Do you have to spend increasing amounts of class time, your time, and the child's time to cope with his problem?

7. Be alert to such passive daydreaming patterns as:

a) Staring at his book or homework while emotionally he is miles away in fantasyland.

b) Gazing at the teacher, or even a peer, with a relatively blank look.

c) Entrancing himself by fixating his attentions on a fly on the wall, the hands on the clock, or the movement of a tree blown by the wind.

8. Don't overlook what is being written or drawn on paper or on the blackboard. Often, the areas of fantasy appear in pictures projected by the student. If drawings appear consistently, they

should be interpreted by a school specialist. He will be able to determine in what areas the child needs support and help. Such pictures are frequently key sources of information as to whether severe emotional problems are emerging.

9. When excessive daydreaming is involved, positive action for its control should be instituted. It is axiomatic that every organism continuously attempts to stabilize itself within its environment. Therefore, as soon as possible, help the child in his personal efforts to evolve a healthy adjustment to the realistic world around him.

Use your checklists to determine whether the patterns of fantasizing are increasing, decreasing, fluctuating, or changing.

DETERMINING TO WHAT EXTENT A CHILD IS BECOMING A "SPECIAL CASE"

While it is usual for a boy or girl to live occasionally in a world of fantasy, there is a fine line between normal patterns and the beginnings of "special case" behavior.

Actually, this line shifts from individual to individual. It is seldom that one specific incident or trauma will push a child into abnormal fantasy. Usually, a continuous reinforcement of pressure is required.

However, the behavior pattern can drift into the extremely neurotic or psychotic with relatively little warning and relatively unmotivated. This is especially true if the child is not too verbal or visibly active in his make-believe world.

Pinpoint the tendency of a child to withdraw further and further from reality. Such a tendency, like a silver thread, runs through the warp and woof in most areas of mental ill health.

A valid diagnosis must be made by a specialist. Your organized, written, dated notations or checklists will be of inestimable value in securing this diagnosis. Here are your guidelines in determining whether you have a "special case":

1. Is the pattern characterized by excessive daydreaming at specific times or places?

- When?
- Where?
- How long?
- How deep?

2. Does it continuously appear when the child is under the same type of pressure? Watch the pressures relating to subject matter, time of day, and involvement of certain individuals.

3. Does the escape mechanism appear to be fostered by anyone, or any group, closely associated with the child?

- Parents?
- Peers?
- Siblings?
- Neighbors?
- Authorities?
- Others?

4. Is the fantasy close to the possible reality? Is it completely apart from rationality? Is there a combination? One child may be lost in thought about driving a car, a reality that is obtainable; another may fantasize being a fairy, flying from mountain top to mountain top, an irrational musing.

5. Can you predict the fluctuations?

6. Are they keeping pace with the child's maturation level? A younger child may want to imagine himself an elf, while an older child may visualize himself as a pilot.

7. Is the amount of fantasizing increasing? Is the depth and the extent of this behavior pattern becoming greater?

8. Is the child becoming a more and more disruptive force?

- To himself?
- To others?
- In the classroom?
- On the playground?

9. Do you find it increasingly difficult to return him to the realities of the immediate situation?

Don't hesitate to identify a potential "special case" in the area of fantasizing. It is better to be too early than too late. Little, if any, harm can be done to the child by pinpointing him, if you keep your findings confidential. On the other hand, much good can be accomplished by initiating early counseling and supportive corrective action.

HOW TO HANDLE THE CHILD WHO HAS BECOME A "SPECIAL CASE"

Two courses of positive action are open to you in helping the child whose excessive fantasy has made him a "special case."

- Take positive counseling action. You then assist him in facing reality more effectively. As his security increases and his need to run from fear-producing situations decreases, he returns to his normal behavior pattern.

• Work optimistically, day by day, even though his condition may continue to deteriorate. He will either slowly begin to return to normal, or reach a point where professional help will be the most feasible solution.

Referrals in this area—unless the "special case" is seriously endangering himself or others—will usually require considerable time from initiation to a successful disposition.

GUIDELINES AS YOU COUNSEL THE CHILD WHO HAS BECOME A "SPECIAL CASE"

1. Although in elementary school much learning involves the use of make-believe, never overlook the opportunity to relate it to life. Even games that utilize creative fantasy have as an ultimate goal the bettering of individual and interpersonal relations in the environment in which the child lives.

2. Use group dynamics to help the "special case" face reality.

Gina might say, "I can fly like Peter Pan," and Timothy shoots down her fantasy balloon by saying, "Maybe you can fly in a plane or a helicopter, but *not* like Peter Pan." Small prods and pressures from the group help not only Gina, but each individual present to differentiate between daydreaming and actuality.

3. Help a child talk about his fantasies, either individually or in a group. Train him to interpret, analyze, and recognize them for what they are. Constructive daydreaming motivates future accomplishment. Destructive daydreaming compounds the present ills.

4. Use play activity, verbalization, and similar routines to help the "special case" gain insight into what he is doing and why he is doing it. Role-playing is especially productive where each individual plays the part of another and tries to imitate how that person feels, thinks, and talks.

5. Stress to the child that his life's goals are accomplished by concentration, hard work, study, etc. Every minute spent in an imaginative world cuts down the amount of time he has available to attain what he wishes.

6. Differentiate between thoughtful planning and listless fantasy.

7. Above all, be honest. Tell the child what is actually happening, what he is doing, and what the results will be.

Keep the discussion in the realistic present. "Johnny, stay with us; don't drift away. Do your arithmetic now, I know you can keep up with the others."

"Sally, are you aware that you didn't hear one word that was said? Come back from dreamland! Finish your writing and we'll all go out and folk dance."

8. Try to bring out into the open, preferably in an individual way, the fears, hopes, and problems that may underlie the child's need to pretend. These problems may not be solvable by you or the child. Discussing them may help the "special case" in his fight to face reality and regain his emotional equilibrium.

9. Physically separate children indulging in excessive reverie Verbalize the need for them to play with boys and girls who do not live in the dream world that they occupy.

10. Wherever possible, give the child realistic and socially acceptable defenses against the fantasies and exaggerations he finds in daily life.

As an example, every toothpaste advertised on television cannot be the best. They all have something, and the form their advertisement takes is their way of attempting to get their product accepted by the public.

11. Each child is different; each child's fantasies are different. Each "special case" is, in reality, a specific problem and must be handled individually.

Utilize your own empathy and intuitive understanding. Help the entire class, as well as the "special case," to distinguish between unacceptable fantasy and acceptable escape mechanisms.

Use daydreaming as a creative force!

13

Little Thumbsuckers and Nailbiters Need Love

Unacceptable chronic behavior patterns give significant clues that deep internal tensions exist within a child.

Oral gratification is a basic need for every human being. Every infant derives much satisfaction from sucking any object which is put into his mouth. This is true whether it is a nipple, a teething ring, or a thumb and finger. He is beginning to savor the pleasure of oral activities.

As he matures into childhood, and later into adulthood, he reaches out for additional oral pleasures. These will include eating, drinking, sucking, chewing, talking, kissing, mouth gestures, and possibly smoking.

A baby's world is self-centered. He himself originates much of his own personal gratification. Through thumbsucking he is able to fulfill partially, and in a normal way, his need for self-love.

Love is possibly the most important thing required by the human animal. Without a mature self-love, he is unable to give love to anyone else.

The inner exchange of love is almost essential for survival. Therefore, the child who is deprived of love will experience deep internal tensions. He will struggle to get love. To fulfill this need, he may adopt almost any technique.

Some techniques are more easily pinpointed than others. Some are more socially acceptable than others. Some create problems for the individual, others resolve problems. All fulfill needs. Two of these techniques are thumbsucking and nailbiting. Both are seen commonly in the elementary school classroom. Both are abnormal at this age level, from kindergarten on. Both are symptoms of unfulfilled emotional needs.

It is easy to say, "Louise, don't suck your thumb!" or "Elmer, stop that nailbiting!" but it is difficult for the child to do this unless his desperate need is fulfilled in other ways. In nearly all children with a case history of this behavior pattern, there is a strong syndrome of inadequacy and insecurity. Such a child needs an immense amount of support that he equates with adequate security and with assurance of love.

If Louise does stop sucking her thumb, something must take its place. Unless a positive mature way to satisfy this need is developed, she will merely adopt another symptom. She may rub her nose, chew a pencil, carry a pet doll or other toy, twist her hair, etc., and thus achieve the same satisfaction as before.

Similarly, if Elmer can stop his nailbiting, he may start scratching his head until it bleeds, begin cracking his knuckles, or turn to mutilating himself with a pen or pencil. He may even attract more than his share of physical hurts on the playground.

Thus, both Louise and Elmer are still coping with unfulfilled emotional needs. In addition, they are giving significant clues that deep internal tensions exist.

Symptoms of internal pressures may appear suddenly. Such was the case with Rita. Rita had ceased thumbsucking at about the age of three. However, as she entered the second grade, her world was shattered. An only child, she was presented with a complicated set of situations following the birth of a baby brother.

Regression to a more secure infantile stage resulted, and Rita reverted to the security of her earlier thumbsucking. Her action was, in reality, a warning signal that she was not getting the warmth, understanding, and love that her particular personality demanded.

Her teacher, Mrs. Muriel T., identified the pattern of regression. Once the symptom was recognized, there was no difficulty in discovering what was troubling the child. Mrs. T. was able to help Rita by use of a three-fold program:

- She gave Rita extra attention and thus became a "good strong mother substitute."

- She provided opportunities for Rita to be the center of her group.
- She was able, by verbal counseling, to develop within Rita a sense of pride and accomplishment in having a baby brother. Slowly, Rita returned to the normal maturity level of a second grader.

Thumbsucking at the elementary school level is always a signal that emotional problems exist. Solutions to and resolutions of the problems are not easy or perhaps even possible at this point. However, when heeded properly, the alert teacher will be able to support and help the child mature at his own speed.

In general, nailbiting may be looked upon as an addition to thumbsucking. It is basically a masochistic act, whereby the individual is chewing or eating himself. This symptom is associated with thumbsucking in that both originate from deep-seated tensions and appear in the oral area.

Nailbiting becomes a punishment because the child is, in effect, hurting himself, and is thus reinforcing a negative form of self-love.

Unless the cause can be pinpointed and resolved, the symptom of nailbiting will be continued or transferred to some other type of more or less socially acceptable behavior or socially unacceptable behavior.

Through thumbsucking, nailbiting, and similar patterns, the child is able to achieve three important goals. He is able to satisfy his deep internal needs for:

- Love and self-warmth.
- Self-punishment for being inadequate.
- Regression to an earlier developmental level where he felt more secure.

Such behavior patterns are normal in the elementary school child if they appear infrequently.

If a child is still continually sucking his thumb and/or biting his nails, at this point in his development, there is still a severe underlying, unresolved problem.

GUIDELINES TO CONTROL THUMBSUCKING AND NAILBITING IN THE NORMAL CHILD

1. Never overlook thumbsucking and nailbiting. Both are symptoms of emotional maladjustment.

2. Whether or not the entire class is involved, counsel each child on an individual basis. This is done slowly, perhaps only a few minutes a day, in which you allow the child to verbalize to you his anxieties and fears. As you understand his needs, your direct and indirect support helps him understand his needs too. As his security within his environment increases, his self-destruction patterns tend to decrease.

3. Never discuss an individual child's symptoms as a public problem. The possibility that this could be a subconscious release of your own hostility is too strong. Too frequently such action will be interpreted as a form of teasing or punishment, and may well increase the severity of the child's symptoms.

4. Through individual counseling, attempt to discover the origin of the pressures. Whether imaginary or not, they are very real to any child.

5. Through verbalization and reasoning, it is often possible to decrease the numbers and amounts of pressures, and thus help the child cope with his environment.

6. Help him accept and live with the problems he cannot change, particularly those originating in his home.

7. Aid him in controlling threatening situations from which he can be removed or can remove himself. Orient him to the values of either changing his immediate environment or having one in authority change it.

For example, he can be taken out of a group situation on the playground, or his seat can be changed in the classroom. He can, in effect, decide whom he will choose as friends after school.

8. Encourage him to detach himself or to limit his relationships in situations or with persons who produce physical and emotional pressures on him.

9. Through direct and indirect group counseling, in the classroom and on the playground, introduce and show the value of techniques for overcoming pressures. Interpret what is happening in the individual during his interpersonal relations. Use basic activities that will include:

   a) Games or playacting, such as hitting, running, building, finger painting, clay modeling.
   b) Verbal arguing under strict control, rules, and regulations.
   c) Interpretative ventilating of grievances, either individually or in groups.

d) Competitive sports, games, drills, spelling bees.

e) Reasoning and verbalizing about logical methods of reducing pressures, fears, and anxieties to realistic size and proportion.

EVALUATING THE COURSES OF ACTION

• Recognize that thumbsucking and nailbiting at the elementary school level are abnormal and socially unacceptable forms of behavior. They do, however, fill a child's need and will only disappear when that need is fulfilled in a more appropriate way.

• Take note of these symptoms as indicators of deep underlying tension. Such symptoms should not be condoned. They must, however, be accepted, at least temporarily, pending the growth of emotional maturity.

• Avoid punishment and condemnation. Such negative actions will do nothing to help the child overcome his anxieties and unacceptable symptoms. In many instances, such acts on the part of authority or peers will increase the depth of the disturbance and delay any therapeutic progress that may be occurring.

• Never forget that public attention, whether by authority or peers, tends to increase the underlying tensions with overall negative results. This is extremely important as irreparable emotional damage often occurs when a child is held up to what he may evaluate as ridicule and condemnation. Don't let it happen in your classroom.

• Give warmth, understanding, and forms of love which will aid the child in fulfilling his needs for self-love. This should be done in ways and with interpretations from you, so that he learns gratifying ways to achieve the same type of love-satisfaction from others.

• You may well choose to do nothing about this type of problem until it has reached extreme proportions. Its handling requires the giving of a tremendous amount of subtle and positive help in a completely unemotional, consistent, and supportive manner.

• Continuous and careful use of your checklists will orient you and your administration to the complexities of this type of "special case." Such written records will help you gauge progress or regression. In addition, your notations will provide a basis for referral, and will give invaluable assistance to a specialist in his overall evaluation of the case and its disposition.

It is important to note that seldom is any individual child referred for professional help for problems of nailbiting and thumbsucking of and by themselves. However, this syndrome is found in a large number of cases referred for other reasons, such as extreme anti-social acts, emotional withdrawal, depression, acute anxiety with physical symptoms, etc.

THE CHARACTERISTICS OF THE "SPECIAL CASE"

Apparently, the more advanced the culture, and the more prevalent the tensions, the greater the incidence of thumbsucking and nailbiting.

Often, as in the case of Rita, the tension is external, easily pinpointed, and can be overcome within a relatively short period of time.

On the other hand, many cases involve the individual's personality and his own efforts to cope with himself, his society, and the ever-changing situations he encounters.

For example, Miriam is an outgoing and well-liked fifth grader. She dresses well, plays the piano, and is one of the best students in her class. She comes from a fine and privileged home. Miriam has always received support, understanding, and love.

From all apparent observations, there is nothing in her environment that would indicate trouble. However, Miriam consistently bites all ten nails down to the quick. Although completely aware of the problem and ashamed of her hands, she has been unable to stop nailbiting.

What is the difficulty? Basically, it is deep within the child, and although no one else demands it, she personally puts pressure on herself to succeed far above what anyone else expects of her. Subconsciously, she is unable to accept herself as she really is. Self-punishment through nailbiting is the result.

Miriam's behavior problems harm no one but herself. Actually, for a satisfactory resolution of her behavior patterns, Miriam needs extensive therapy. However, the reality of the situation is that since she is creating problems for no one but herself, she is not likely to receive professional help until she is old enough to initiate it on her own volition. At this point, her greatest support will be from a wise and understanding teacher who attempts to take the pressures off Miriam by showing her that success in our society is not solely dependent upon being first in her class, in her peer group struggle, or even in her social world.

In pinpointing the characteristics of the child with a problem of thumbsucking or nailbiting, never trust your empirical judgment. Internal pressures are not easily delineated.

GUIDELINES FOR PINPOINTING THE CHARACTERISTICS OF THE "SPECIAL CASE"

1. Behavior patterns in thumbsucking and nailbiting evolve slowly.

2. Even when the causes, especially if external, can be determined and eliminated, the possibility is strong that if a change is forced upon the child, he will fill his need by adopting a new set of tensions and symptoms.

3. In severe cases, the symptoms may proceed to the point where thumbsucking is destroying the tooth structure and the shape of the jaw, as well as creating callouses, lesions, and disfigurations of the thumb.

Nailbiting may be so acute that there is constant infection. Bleeding and scabs may appear on the skin surrounding the nail.

4. Bear in mind that all forms of thumbsucking and nailbiting are, in reality, only symptoms, and that treatment of symptoms is rarely effective. The pressures causing these symptoms must be resolved, decreased, or changed if the child is to function normally.

DETERMINING TO WHAT EXTENT A CHILD IS BECOMING A "SPECIAL CASE"

Thumbsucking and nailbiting are basically techniques of releasing anxiety through physical means. For this reason, it is imperative that the problem always be regarded as significant and potentially serious. Use these guidelines:

1. At the elementary school level, every child with the behavior patterns of thumbsucking and nailbiting must be considered a "special case."

2. Watch for fluctuations of the behavior patterns. Keep a written record on your checklists to ascertain whether such fluctuations exist and if they are increasing or decreasing in severity and in frequency.

3. Does the child appear to be hurting himself physically? Is medical attention needed?

4. Is the symptom pattern affected by pressures that you can readily observe? That you can effectively regulate or control?

5. Are the pressures so well hidden and undefined that it is impossible to pinpoint them?

6. Can you determine the origin of pressures that appear to be creating the child's tensions? Are they child-oriented? Home-oriented? Society-oriented? School-oriented?

7. Do specific school situations seem to lessen or increase the pressures?

8. Do you have reason to believe that the child is suffering from lack of warmth, understanding, love, and/or oral gratification?

9. Is he demanding too much of himself? Setting unobtainable goals? Does there appear to be a need for him to punish himself?

To answer these questions, develop checklists to suit your needs. Through them, you may move, step by step, to determine the extent of the problem and to seek a realistic solution. Your chronological notations will also aid you in evaluating your success and your capabilities as you help each child find solutions that enable him to establish a more satisfactory adjustment to his society.

Never underestimate the seriousness of this type of "special case" behavior pattern. Such symptoms of poor adjustment are becoming more and more prevalent in our society.

Little thumbsuckers and nailbiters are in need of love. There is no doubt that they are suffering emotionally. If they are physically hurting themselves, medical and psychological help are urgent.

HOW TO HANDLE THE CHILD WHO HAS BECOME A "SPECIAL CASE"

Even though you may find it impossible to determine the causes and the extent of the problems that create the symptoms of thumbsucking and nailbiting, there are many techniques available to you to help the child. Use these guidelines:

1. Accept the "special case" as a person and human being in dire need of love.

2. The need for self-love is basic. Help the child establish acceptable patterns of self-love. These should include:

• Pride in himself and what he does.

- Acceptance of his own capabilities and limitations.
- Self-forgiveness for real and imagined deficiencies.
- Ability to give as well as to receive love, warmth, and understanding.

3. Remember that a child's world is self-centered. Therefore, it is very human for him to:

- Always want his own way.
- Satisfy his basic needs and drives at the expense of someone else.
- Be completely unaware that he has ridden roughshod over the feelings of another.

4 Use the directive and non-directive counseling procedures in your approach. Help each "special case" become aware of how to relate his needs for self-love to the same needs of others.

5. Orient him to the socially acceptable pattern of "give and take" when it comes to fulfilling his own physical, intellectual, and emotional needs as well as the needs of others.

6. Help him verbalize, insofar as he can, the pressures in his life. Persuade him to discuss the fears and tensions he feels. Utilize individual and group counseling techniques. Help him accept the reality that others, adults as well as peers, experience many of the same pressures, fears, and tensions.

7. Aid him in discovering what part his own imagination, intellect, and feelings, as well as those of persons around him, play in establishing his own actions. Help him to:

- Face reality.
- Overcome unfounded feelings of inferiority and insecurity.
- Use his imagination as a constructive rather than a destructive force.

8. Never forget—and never allow the child to forget—that the harsh realities of pressures, tensions, and fears are always with us. Help him develop acceptable defense mechanisms that cope with these realities. Be alert to the symptoms which indicate when he is not effectively handling these realities.

9. Use all the facilities available to you, the peer group, the administration, the family, and the physical surroundings, to give the child support in maturing emotionally.

10. Seek constantly to develop new ways to resolve the problem. What will work in one case will not necessarily succeed in another.

What will be effective at one time may be ineffective at another. Discard those techniques which prove to be of little help to you.

11. Avoid the use of punishment and the unfavorable spotlight of adverse public attention.

12. Use your checklists to record and to comment upon the progress of each "special case."

Be alert to the need for referral. Generally, unless the child is creating a disturbance in the class or at home, he will not be referred for professional help. Neither will he be removed from your classroom situation.

This does not mean that the child is not a "special case" or that he does not need help. However, since it is always the "wheel that squeaks that gets the grease," this particular child is usually overlooked. Yet, he may be more apt to respond favorably to your counseling than perhaps ninety per cent of the other "special cases" discussed in this book.

Even when there is no visible improvement, little thumbsuckers and nailbiters will profit immeasurably from the relationship of a teacher who is willing to give them time, warmth, understanding, and interpretative support. Maturation will occur even though it is not immediately apparent.

Above all, little thumbsuckers and nailbiters need love.

14

Fire-Players and
Little Fire-Setters

Nothing fascinates like fire.

Every child is fascinated by fire. He wants to play and experiment with it. This fascination is normal.

Like his ancestors, the elementary school child is satisfying many basic drives, including the needs to:

- Find security.
- Explore, discover, and experiment.
- Control, build, and destroy.
- Acquire knowledge and satisfy curiosity.
- Express himself and show off.

Therefore, it is to be anticipated that you, the elementary school teacher, will find some pupils carrying and experimenting with matches and combustible materials. This is normal.

Fascination with fire dates to prehistoric times. Discovery of how to control fire was perhaps the greatest milestone of man's advancement in civilization. Controlled fire nurtured man's person by providing warmth, making his food more palatable, and symbolizing the center of comfortable existence. Fire has always played a key role in the family, tribal, religious, and governmental life of man. Ritual, tradition, and law grew up concerning where, when, why, in what way, and by whom, fire was to be lighted and extinguished.

Today, even more than in the past, we are surrounded by controls relating to fire. Restrictions, such as "no smoking," "no trash burning," or "no campfires without permit," are necessary for our survival. Fire today, as in the past, poses one of the greatest threats to the existence of man, and is the basis of two major fears:

1. Without fire, man, his family, and his possessions may perish.
2. Fire may destroy all man owns, his loved ones, and himself.

The patterns of uncontrolled fire-setting, such as arson, incendiarism, and pyromania, are encountered even at the elementary school level.

By the time a child has reached kindergarten, he has a fairly well-formed concept of the dangers of fire and what it can do for and against him. However, he may be having difficulty fulfilling his needs and controlling his drives for fire-playing. By observing and analyzing his behavior patterns, you may pinpoint whether he is acting in socially acceptable ways or whether he is tending toward the adoption of anti-social patterns of fire-setting, such as:

- Arson—purposefully setting fire to buildings, trees, etc.
- Incendiarism—willfully destroying property by fire.
- Pyromania—feeling compelled to start fires.

Other anti-social behavior patterns may be involved with fire-setting, such as juvenile delinquency, excessive hostility, mental and emotional incompetency. Bed wetting and sexually related problems may also appear as there is often a relationship between these emotionally oriented disturbances and patterns of uncontrolled fire-setting.

GUIDELINES TO CONTROL FIRE-SETTING IN THE NORMAL CHILD

1. Recognize that every child is fascinated with fire. He is interested in lighting a fire, putting it out, experimenting with what will and will not burn.

2. Accept and give him ample opportunity to learn and to experiment. Such interests are normal. Attempt to discover means to satisfy his needs in socially acceptable ways.

3. Utilize birthdays, Christmas, Easter, etc., to give you an opportunity to allow fire-setting (lighting the candles) and fire-extinguishing (blowing out the candles). Actually, every child can take turns lighting and extinguishing candles.

4. When time and facilities permit, allow the child to burn trash

in the incinerator, to start the campfire on a school outing, or to perform simple general science experiments that involve combustion and pyrotechnics before the class. When the situation is such that home, school, or community clean-up projects are underway, and trash, leaves, and other rubbish is to be burned, encourage the children to participate. Through this outlet, each child fulfills his need to destroy, to burn, and to satisfy his curiosity as to how fire consumes. Likewise, his need to participate in building a better community through these supervised efforts is accomplished.

5. Stress consistently the importance of caring for and controlling fire. Emphasize the natural and the man-made laws that are involved in the utilization of fire.

6. Use every opportunity in a learning situation to increase each child's knowledge about fire. Include fire drills, news events, and field trips to fire departments and police stations.

7. Whenever possible and practical, counsel the parents. Help them visualize the value of providing their child occasions to start the fire in the fire-place, campfire, bar-b-que, and furnace. With parental supervision, the child learns the ways to fuel and refuel various types of fires.

For example, Ken S. was a normal third grader. Mrs. Anna P., his teacher, noticed Ken's pockets were continually filled with matches, paper scraps, and small pieces of wood. Mrs. P. suspected that Ken probably enjoyed starting and fueling small fires, although no one had ever caught him. Since the potential was there, she decided to approach the subject at parent conference time.

"Yes, Mrs. P., Ken has started a couple of fires in the backyard," Ken's mother volunteered. "We've spanked him, but that hasn't been too effective."

With a little parental counseling, Ken's mother was advised to continue discipline, but to change from corporal punishment, which was ineffective, to limiting by various times and amounts, the play activities that Ken liked most. Reward him when he handles fire right; restrict him when he doesn't. She was urged to try additional and supportive techniques. She let Ken light the gas stove for each meal, and permitted him to burn trash in the incinerator. In return, Ken left his matches and combustibles in their proper places at home. His drive to set additional and unauthorized fires was controlled.

In Ken's case, a little understanding channelled his needs into useful functions and resolved what might have become a "special case."

8. Due to the extreme danger of playing with fire, it is impossible to condone any type of fire-setting, other than those completely supervised and controlled. Infractions must be immediately handled with normal disciplinary action.

9. Punishment with understanding and dignity must be impartially and consistently administered. It should come immediately; however, counseling is an essential measure, combined with discipline. Explain the way, the possible consequences, and the limitations involved.

EVALUATING THE COURSES OF ACTION

• Playing with fire does not make a child a "special case." Accept the fact that such play will occur. However, take positive action immediately in each instance.

• Use discipline coupled with counseling. Discipline alone may keep most little fire-players from participating in dangerous or anti-social situations involving fire. The insight that counseling supplies, however, will help each child cope with his personal problems. In the process, he will find more adequate and more suitable outlets for his needs and drives.

• When the behavior patterns of a child indicate the possibility of his being a little fire-player or fire-setter, do not postpone seeking additional help. Inform the parents, your principal, other teachers, and your school's professional consultants. A continued repetition of fire-setting patterns is frequently an indicator of deep personality disturbances.

• When the pattern of fire-playing and fire-setting is repeated, consider the possibilities of a "special case" developing. Use your checklists to aid you. They become a written record that may be the foundation of any future action.

THE CHARACTERISTICS OF THE "SPECIAL CASE"

When your empirical feelings and cursory evaluation of your checklists indicate that perhaps you have a "special case" involving little fire-players and fire-setters, take immediate steps to determine the extent, width, depth, and scope of the problem.

Ask yourself two questions: First, "Do I have a simple problem of a child playing with fire, a 'special case' that I can cope with?" And second, "Is this a 'special case' that needs immediate administrative attention and professional help?"

Joey, a fifth grader, has been a disciplinary problem to each of his previous teachers. Several times a year there had been "trips" to the principal for his anti-social actions involving fighting, minor sexual behavior problems, and playing with matches or small fires. Joey's parents had cooperated with the school. His father was a military officer and a strict disciplinarian at home. Unfortunately, the family had moved frequently, so that no school had a complete history of Joey's behavior patterns. His parents indicated that he was restless at home and had periodic bouts of enuresis (bed wetting). Twice, he had set fires in a closet and then extinguished them. He was rebellious to both parents, especially his mother.

Joey set a fire behind one of the school storage buildings. The principal caught him, extinguished the small conflagration, and summoned the police. The juvenile authorities released Joey to his parents, with strong suggestions that they seek professional help for the child before he became involved in a more serious crime.

Joey was a "special case." He had been one for several years. However, due to many factors—moving, poor follow-up, lack of continuous records, and so forth—no teacher had pinpointed this problem. Yet several characteristics of the "special case" had been present for some time:

- He had been playing with fires in unacceptable patterns at home and at school.
- There was a continuous problem of aggression and hostility toward others.
- Difficulties and problems with peers involving sexual areas had occurred.
- Enuresis existed.

Everyone who wets the bed does not set fires. Bed wetting, however, especially after a child has reached school age, is a strong indicator of emotional instability. In a large percentage of cases of incendiarism, the individual has been a problem bed wetter. Indeed, the tendency toward pyromania is considered by many to be a urethra-erotic character trait.

Whether a child like Joey, when first identified as a "special case," can be helped by you, the teacher; or whether he is allowed to persist in his anti-social behavior patterns until the community must take action, depends upon five factors:

- Your capacities (emotional, physical, and time) to counsel effectively.
- The facilities of the school.
- The cooperation of the parents.
- The child's limitations.
- The community resources available for referral.

If your written and empirical evaluations indicate that a problem of fire-setting exists, watch for the characteristics of the "special case."

GUIDELINES FOR PINPOINTING THE CHARACTERISTICS OF THE "SPECIAL CASE"

1. Accept the fact that fire, and playing with fire, fascinates all children. Recognize, however, that such experimentation with fire must be done in a well controlled situation with constant supervision.

2. Is there a strong unfulfilled need to hurt, to destroy, to control, and/or to engage in activity that irritates or upsets authority and the status quo? Is the child able to release his hostility in acceptable ways?

3. If one child or a group of children are overly concerned about fire or combustibles that normally are associated with fire-setting, or if they seem to be preoccupied with fire, they are displaying symptoms of a potential "special case" of little fire-players and fire-setters.

4. Does there appear to be an increase in the incidence level of fire-oriented activity?

5. Are there personality problems in the urethra-erotic area, such as enuresis?

6. Does the child have difficulty in his interpersonal relations with others? Does he often appear at war with himself, his peers, and superiors? Is he in a constant state of rebellion?

7. Has his activity involved in fire-setting been open and obviously exploited? Or has it been covert with the devious indications that he is well aware of its unacceptability?

Any or all of these guidelines may appear without the child becoming a "special case" of fire-playing. However, they are strong indicators that a "special case" may be developing.

DETERMINING TO WHAT EXTENT A CHILD IS BECOMING A "SPECIAL CASE"

Actually, the first time you uncover an activity involving fire-setting, the possibilities are high that a "special case" may exist. Unlike many anti-social acts of emotionally troubled children, the incendiary behavior patterns of little fire-players and fire-setters cannot be ignored or tolerated. A strong likelihood exists that by the time you discover such activity, the child will already have a history of anti-social behavior patterns that indicate he is a "special case."

Like the child with unacceptable sexual behavior patterns, the little fire-player is aware that as far as authority figures are concerned, his fire-setting spawns trouble. Therefore, he becomes adept at hiding such activity. Frequently, this child is only discovered when an uncontrolled blaze appears and he is trapped.

GUIDELINES IN DETERMINING WHETHER A "SPECIAL CASE" IS DEVELOPING

• Is there any evidence that this fire-setting or playing with fire is a repetitious act? In other words, are you sure when you observed and questioned him, that this was the first time the potenially dangerous act had occurred? A recurrence indicates a "special case."

• Discipline has not terminated the activity of playing with fire.

• Normal counseling involving the individual, as well as the class, about the problems of fire and fire-setting, the do's and don't's of lighting and putting out fires, has not been effective in eliminating fire-setting patterns.

• Your intuition and previous experience tell you that a "special case" exists, and that you are not getting "all of the facts."

TECHNIQUES FOR FIRM DISCIPLINARY CONTROL

Direct discipline, of course, involves both punishment and reward. The concept is to reinforce, either positively or negatively, the behavioral pattern you desire in your "special case," or to discourage and diminish the patterns you desire to eliminate or curb. Punishment becomes the loss of something the child wants. It may be comfort, status, or privileges. Reward is attaining the fulfillment or partial fulfillment of emotional, physical, and social needs and desires.

Firm disciplinary control can originate from five sources:

- You, the teacher.
- Society—the law, mores, religious codes, etc.
- Immediate authority figures—administration, parents, organizations, and group leaders.
- Peers—the society of the child in his immediate environment—classmates, members of his social, religious, and neighborhood groups.
- The individual himself.

The techniques you develop will utilize all sources. To be most effective, direct discipline must come as soon as possible after the act. Counseling occurs most favorably when the crisis is past and all parties can talk, think, share, and seek solutions without undue emotional fervor. Direct discipline may also involve keeping the child after school, changing his seat, taking away or awarding special honors or demerits, assigning unpleasant or highly desired tasks (as the group that helps the teacher on a job or the group that is the last to go out for recess). Discipline must fit the child, the crime, and the situation. Most of us make the mistake of using too much "ammunition" at one time. This puts the child in a hopeless situation. As an example, Jean talks and interrupts the teacher. After repeated warnings of possible action, the teacher takes away her privilege to help pass out the workbooks that day. An hour later, Jean loses the privilege for the following day. After the third disciplinary action, Jean's punishment is projected so far into the future that its desired effect is lost. It would have been more judicious if the teacher had revoked the privilege for only an hour. Her supply of "ammunition" would still be intact. The desired disciplinary effect would then be in the immediate present.

HOW TO HANDLE THE CHILD WHO HAS BECOME A "SPECIAL CASE"

As evaluation of your checklists pinpoints the "special case" of fire-playing and fire-setting, you will be aware that positive action toward helping the child, as well as protecting the person and property of others, is urgent. Four courses of action are open to you:

1. Do nothing. Wait until property is destroyed or someone is hurt and the juvenile authorities are forced to take action.

2. Use all the direct discipline at your disposal or at the disposal of your administration. If this is effective, you will need nothing further than your normal supportive counseling techniques. If not, then you must decide what additional steps you are willing to take.

3. Attempt both direct and indirect counseling to assist the child to:

   a) Understand himself, his needs, and his drives.
   b) Help him seek and adjust to socially satisfying outlets for these drives.
   c) Conform to the restrictions, limitations, and controls his society places on fire-setting.

4. Give careful consideration to the possible involvement of other sources for help.

   a) This referral is urgent if:
      (1) The problem is past your control.
      (2) All the means at your disposal for resolving the problem have been exhausted.
   b) Refer this "special case" to:
      (1) Your principal and school specialists for further professional evaluation and help.
      (2) The child's parents for help at home.
      (3) Governmental agencies or private facilities available for this type of "special case."

GUIDELINES AS YOU COUNSEL THE CHILD WHO HAS BECOME A "SPECIAL CASE"

1. In a "special case" involving little fire-players or fire-setters, be aware that you are literally "playing with fire." Time is of the essence. Immediate positive measures must be taken.

2. In the school situation, the "special case" who plays with and sets fires cannot be tolerated. Your first action will of necessity involve discipline, for no other reason than that, when the activity is discovered, protection of the individual or individuals and the safeguard of public or private property is imperative.

3. Counseling should augment discipline. Counseling may be both direct and indirect. It may be with the individual, as well as

with the group. How your counseling is put into effect will depend upon the situation. Time, amenability of the "special case," involvement, and immediate danger are primary consideratons.

4. The environment surrounding the fire-setting must be considered in establishing the tone of counseling. Where this unacceptable act occurred is important: Was it at home, or on the way to or from school? How the problem arose; if one or more "special cases" are involved; and whether strong "leader" or "follower" patterns exist, will affect your techniques of counseling. When the problem consists of only one or two "special cases," individual counseling will be most effective.

As you uncover the possible causes, the reasons, the pressures on the child, the temperament and personality of those involved, your course of action may shift. Flexibility in your patterns of discipline and techniques of counseling is essential to help each "special case."

5. The time you have available for counseling this type of "special case" is a meaningful factor as to whether you will succeed or fail. It is always possible that any satisfactory solution may just plain require more of your personal time for counseling and support than it is possible for you to contribute. Many teachers just do not have the additional leeway in their schedule.

Fortunate, indeed, are you if you have the spare moments so necessary to handle any but the least involved "special cases." However, sometimes just a little support and a little latitude in allowing the child to "talk out" or "play out" his feelings will open the door.

6. The amenability of the "special case" to your counseling, to group pressures, and to a desire for conforming to the socially acceptable, is important to any successful counseling with this "special case."

7 Your counseling must consider the child's need to control, to destroy, and to build. His hostility to himself and to authority and those around him has to be ventilated and released in acceptable ways. He must be allowed to express himself, satisfy his curiosity, explore and experiment. As he does these, he needs support, interpretation, and direction from you.

8. The depth of involvement of the problem in the "special case" of little fire-setters is important to the success of any counseling program. If the fire-setting patterns are not deeply rooted, and if the behavior patterns are not deeply rooted, and if the behavior pattern is spotty, you should encounter some success. However,

if the child tends to be inflexible with deep-seated and consistent anti-social behavior patterns of fire-setting, success may be tenuous. This is the type of "special case" in which early recognition of the problem is important. Like other "special cases" that involve sexual behavior patterns or involve sexually related syndromes, immediate action is a critical factor. The assistance of a trained professional is urgently needed.

9. In this special case, does an immediate danger exist? Is there a possibility that the juvenile authorities may be involved? If the "special case" is experimenting with explosives, pyrotechnics, or surreptitiously setting fires, probably there is danger not only to individuals, but to property. Such unsupervised or clandestine activity cannot be tolerated. Even though indirect counseling is used, direct disciplinary action must be taken to make sure that at least these dangerous areas in the child's fire-setting patterns are terminated.

10. How effective you the teacher are in handling this "special case" depends also in some respect on your own emotional reactions toward fire. If your feelings are strong, and involve personal fear and guilt, you may find fire-setting and fire-playing a problem you can handle only with discipline. However, if you feel adequate and can help the child act out his emotional drives, you may be very successful in your counseling. Talk about his feelings; actually let him light fires. You probably will achieve far greater results than you anticipated.

11. Playing out the drive to set fires is a type of direct counseling in which the "special case" acts out his needs under a controlled and interpreted situation. It may occur at candle-lighting time at a birthday party, fire-setting time in the home or camp fireplace, or at leaf-burning time in the fall or trash-burning time in his own backyard or the school incinerator. It is most effective, of course, if the parents are able to take such action with the child. However, any well-linked authority figure, such as a scoutmaster, a teacher, or a church or agency group leader involved in hiking and camping activities is in an excellent position to counsel this "special case." You, his primary school teacher, are in the best position to refer, to inform, and to influence others involved in helping this child resolve his problems.

12. Recognize that the "special case" of the little fire-setter probably exhibits many other symptoms of emotional instability.

When such symptoms appear, as excessive bed wetting, overexcitement at going to, seeing, or becoming involved in conflagrations, strongly consider the urgency of an immediate referral for professional evaluation.

Each little fire-setter needs to be as completely aware as possible of his needs and drives. He must recognize that he has a problem. He needs to know what he can and cannot do. He must accept the fact that serious repercussions may follow any of his unacceptable acts of fire-playing. Of necessity, he will find adequate releases that are socially acceptable. If he doesn't, he will eventually be isolated from society. Your discipline, counseling, or referral may help him resolve this problem. Carefully annotated records will make the task easier for everyone involved in resolving this "special case."

15

Liars and Little Cheaters

Survival is the first law of the individual. A child protects himself by presenting his best defenses to the threatening world.

From your evaluation, as a teacher and as an adult, it may be perfectly obvious that a child is fibbing, lying, or cheating. Emotionally and sometimes intellectually, it may not be the least bit obvious to the child.

As an example, Mrs. Smith has just had the blackboard washed. She says, "Please don't write on the blackboard because we're going to use it for a special Thanksgiving drawing." Ten minutes later, Billy is doodling with chalk on one of the corners. Angrily, Mrs. Smith says, "I thought I told you no one was to write on the blackboard."

Billy innocently replies, as he drops the chalk and turns to face his accuser, "I didn't write on the blackboard; I was just making some marks."

From a realistic point of view, Billy grabs at the first available defense mechanism—denial. To him, this isn't lying; he is protecting himself. But to Mrs. Smith, he is an outright, blatant fibber, caught in the act. Actually, it is probably almost impossible at this moment of confrontation to convince this child that he has lied. However, every teacher has the problem of coping almost daily with situations such as this. Billy's reaction is normal. He is attempting to achieve one or more of three goals:

- Protection or defense of his little psyche from attacks by the outside world.

140

- Strengthening his feelings about himself.
- Building up his status in the eyes of those around him.

As the child matures, he becomes more and more aware of reality and of his emotional, mental, and physical relationships with reality. He slowly learns when he is actually misrepresenting a situation through fibbing and lying. This is true whether the misrepresentation is to himself, to his peer environment, or to the adult world around him.

Cheating, like lying, may be a technique to defend the psyche or to protect a real or imagined inadequacy in the child's ability to cope with his environment. Whether in the classroom or on the playground, the unprepared child may need to cheat to minimize what he interprets as his inferiorities and personal inadequacies.

For example, the intellectually gifted individual in the classroom may arrive ill prepared for a specific class. The need to maintain his position may force him to cheat or to lie.

It is difficult to establish a good positive standard for a child when he sometimes sees and hears statements made by important public and government figures turning out to be false. Even the authority figures around him often present information that turns out to be erroneous. This is one of the harsh realities of life in our society.

As a teacher, you can be of inestimable value in strengthening the child's ethical concepts. A certain amount of fibbing, lying, and cheating is normal at the elementary school level. Such actions, properly interpreted by the child and those around him, help him mature, and develop more realistic and socially acceptable techniques of protecting and building up his psyche.

GUIDELINES TO CONTROL LYING AND CHEATING PATTERNS IN THE NORMAL CHILD

1. Fibbing, lying, and cheating are normal and will occur. Thus, it is important to be aware of their existence and of the forms they take.

2. Immediate action on your part will often keep the problem from "ballooning" out of proportion.

As an example, Butch, in the second grade, has just been caught cheating during a spelling quiz. His teacher, Mrs. M., questions him. She is aware that a "do-nothing" attitude can easily establish a poor pattern for Butch as well as for the entire class.

"Did you copy Mary Jane's spelling words? You were looking at her paper."

"No! I didn't do it!" was Butch's normal and defensive response.

This did not convince Mrs. M. However, she accepted his answer and handled this problem, keeping four things in mind:

a) Butch has a strong need to lie and cheat.
b) The entire class was a spectator to the incident.
c) The boy must be allowed some means of saving face.
d) An example must still be given the class that lying and cheating are unacceptable and must be controlled by the individual himself and by the adult authorities.

"I'll take your word that you didn't cheat, but the fact that you turned your head toward Mary Jane's paper will disqualify your test today. Butch, you must conduct yourself so that neither the teacher nor anyone else will misunderstand. Otherwise, like today, they may think you are cheating."

Using this technique, Mrs. M. was immediately in control of the specific situations of Butch's cheating and lying and the reaction of the class to it. She applied discipline and made it adhere. She used the incident as a learning situation as to what would happen in the future. In addition, she used this incident as a group counseling opportunity. Summarizing briefly some of the penalties of lying and cheating, she also pointed out many of the longterm rewards of "doing your own work."

3. Each teacher must "play by ear" the relative value of individual versus group counseling when lying and cheating appear. There is no specific or dogmatic technique for coping with such problems. Each child is unique, and each situation is different. Allowing a child to express his feelings and talk about this problem is most important.

4. You as a teacher must help the child who displays the unacceptable patterns of lying and cheating gain his needed ego support by acquiring socially acceptable techniques and outlets.

5. Do not tolerate or ignore lying and cheating. Otherwise, like the rotten apple in a barrel, it will eventually contaminate everyone in the class.

6. In the long run, the energy expended to cheat or lie uses up

far more of the child's available capacity than patterns of honesty will require. It is important to help a child see that this is true of himself.

7. If a large percentage of the class suddenly appears to be lying or cheating, ask yourself, "What is really happening? What are the underlying dynamics?" A reason or combination of reasons may include factors in the present, or in a former teacher, the school, the playground, the social environment, the peer group or its leadership, or the standards of the child's home or community. The lying and cheating may merely be the symptoms of a deeper conflict, as the attempt to resolve apparently unsolvable problems.

8. Change the supervision and the seating facilities if cheating and lying become disruptive to the learning situation. Similarly, attempt to discover what interrelations exist. Is, for instance, the pattern of the classroom lying and cheating brought to or carried from the playground, classroom, or home?

9. From your empirical observations, do the patterns involving lying and cheating appear to be organized by one or more individuals? Are they spontaneous, depending upon the situation?

10. Is the subject matter responsible for the cheating or lying? Is class work too difficult? Too easy? Uninteresting or repetitious? Are other demands to accomplish at home or at school forcing him into these unacceptable patterns?

11. Are family pressures at home (or lack of pressures) triggering off the child's need to lie or cheat? Can you pinpoint them? Are you in a position to help the child cope with these pressures?

12. There is a line up to which discipline and punishment may effectively control lying and cheating. This line or dividing point is hard to delineate. However, once it is reached, punishment and discipline become ineffective and will only force the child to find better techniques to disguise and hide his anti-social activity.

EVALUATING THE COURSES OF ACTION

• One lie doesn't make a liar, and one offense doesn't make a cheater.

Insofar as possible with the normal child, provide "face-saving outs." Don't label him as a "special case" simply because he meets pressures through resorting to instinctive and protective behavior patterns involving lying or cheating.

• Repeated lying and cheating must be regarded as indicative of a "special case." The child, or children involved need immediate and positive attention. Use a consistent system of reward and punishment. Apply counseling involving support, interpretation, and elimination of temptation. Let him talk to you about his feelings and thus build up his own inner strength to do what he decides is right. Again, I stress, be very careful of labeling such a child, either publicly or privately, as a cheater or liar. Irreparable damage is often caused by just such labeling.

• The inability of a child to discern whether he is telling the truth or not, and whether he is cheating or not, will very frequently pinpoint the seriously disturbed child. Your ability to recognize such a child in his formative elementary school years may be of immeasurable help to him, and also to teachers and administrators who will handle him in the future.

• Use a series of checklists to aid you in determining whether a child is becoming a "special case," and needs your additional help.

THE CHARACTERISTICS OF THE "SPECIAL CASE"

Once you suspect that a child is lying and cheating, watch for the characteristics of the "special case." Use the following guidelines:

1. Keep a record of the frequency and the seriousness of the patterns. The extent of involvement is especially significant.

2. The refinement and the ability with which the child employs his patterns of lying and cheating must be gauged in relation to his developmental and maturity levels.

There is a world of difference, for example, between:

• The child who merely glances at a neighbor's paper.
• The one who copies a friend's homework during recess.
• And the one who premeditatively prepares notes to assist him in a test.

3. The anti-social patterns of lying and cheating may stem from many causes and many sources. Attempt to pinpoint:

• The needs being fulfilled.
• The inadequacies being protected.
• The gains and rewards being attained.

4. Is this "special case" attempting to maintain his status within

his peer group? Endeavoring to meet demanding pressures from home? Or attempting to alleviate his own feelings of inadequacy?

5. From your point of view, is there a steady and discernible increase in the difficulty of controling the lying and cheating? By you the teacher? By the parents? By the child himself? By his peers? By the school authorities?

6. Are the parents involved? Are they sympathetic and cooperative with, or are they hostile to you? To the child? The school? The child's peers? Society in general?

DETERMINING TO WHAT EXTENT A CHILD IS BECOMING A "SPECIAL CASE"

A repeated pattern of lying and cheating should always be regarded as a problem in the classroom and on the playground. It demands immediate attention. Here are your guidelines:

1. Watch for the specific situation of lying and cheating. Does the lying and cheating occur in only one subject, such as math? Does it appear in only one playground activity, such as in competitive games? Does it appear as a consistent pattern in any way?

2. Does the unacceptable activity occur relatively continuously in all the child's activities? Or the group's activities?

3. Is only one child involved, or are several individuals a part of the problem?

4. Are there indications that a "follow the leader" pattern might exist?

5. Your normal routines of testing, games, class exercises, drills, blackboard and homework presentations will be the seedbeds in which lying and cheating activities can germinate and grow. Such daily routines will provide you with clues that will enable you to determine whether a problem exists. As you structure them, they can aid you in delineating the extent of the problem and in determining whether a child is becoming a "special case."

What is the motivation for the cheating? The lying? Does it appear to be:

  a) Intellectual capacity?
  b) Physical anomalies?
  c) Social or emotional immaturity?
  d) Drives from home to succeed?
  e) Lack of concern or care at home?

  f) Family difficulties, such as moving, divorce, illness, death, etc.?
  g) Other factors involving a new school situation?
  h) Need for status?
  i) Need to excel? Need to fail?
  j) Need to conform or follow a leader, especially a poor example?
  k) Need to rebel against authority or society?

To answer these questions, use the checklists you feel best fit your situation. Through them you may move, step by step, to pinpoint the "special case," and to determine the extent of the problem.

Consistent use of your checklists with careful notations will provide you with a firm basis for a positive approach in working with the child who has become a "special case" involving lying and/or cheating.

HOW TO HANDLE THE CHILD WHO HAS BECOME A "SPECIAL CASE"

Unlike many behavior patterns, lying and cheating cannot be tolerated in the classroom or on the playground. Three courses are open to you as you institute positive action toward helping the child:

1. Use only discipline, as in the previous chapter.

2. Combine your discipline with counseling and understanding of the world in which he lives. Attempt to help your "special case" uncover the causes and reasons for his lying and cheating. In addition, show him how to adopt techniques to cope with his anti-social behavior patterns.

3. Be realistic. Accept the fact that you cannot succeed in all cases, for any one of three simple reasons: first, you may not have the capacity (for example, your patience is too thin); second, you may not have the time or inclination; third, in spite of all you can do, your "special case" may be too physically, mentally, or emotionally disturbed to adjust to your normal class routines. Use your checklists as the basis for instituting steps with your administration to obtain the best possible help for the child. This may require transfer to a special class or school. It may even entail referral to private or agency sources for psychological help.

GUIDELINES AS YOU COUNSEL THE CHILD WHO HAS BECOME A "SPECIAL CASE"

1. Use every opportunity in the classroom and on the playground to verbalize with the individual as well as the group. Stress the social and personal difficulties that result from adopting patterns of lying and cheating. Most teachers at one time or another find it necessary to cope with cheating and probable lying. You will have to use supervision and well thought out techniques of discipline. In addition, you would do well to use counseling: Treat the entire incident as a learning situation.

Stress the problems of those who:

- Lie and/or cheat.
- Foster, or make necessary the lying and/or cheating.
- Are influenced or affected by the lying and/or cheating of those around them.

2. It would be unrealistic to assume in your interpersonal relations with your students that lying and cheating are not a part of the world around us. Each of your students knows about some of these harsh realities of life. As you counsel, accept the fact that:

a) Many children are taught to lie and cheat. Somebody else teaches them; circumstances teach them; or, they teach themselves.
b) Regardless of how they learn, they become a "special case," as far as you and the school are concerned.
c) Everyone around the liar and the little cheater is influenced and affected by his behavior patterns.

3 Help the "special case" place in proper perspective the various forms of make-believe which he encounters in films and television.

There is a vast difference between the untruths of fantasy in the entertainment world and the lying and cheating in the classroom situation. Yet it is easy for the individual to rationalize and justify his actions in the world of reality with actions he has observed in television and movie land.

4. Recognize the variations and extenuating circumstances of each situation. However, do not condone, or allow to slip by, incidents of lying or cheating.

To paraphrase an old adage, "Condemn the lying and cheating, but do not condemn the liar or cheater."

When the lying is related to unacceptable sexual behavior patterns, do not hesitate to involve your professional consultants.

5. Depending upon the extent to which his acts are socially acceptable, and regardless of his background and the amount of lying and cheating in the home environment, the "special case" must be counseled about the penalties which may come his way if he continues to lie and cheat.

6 You can help each "special case" develop for himself workable techniques to replace unacceptable patterns of lying about personal situations and family background.

For example, the court had taken David away from his parents and placed him in a foster home. His classmates knew of his troubles and taunted him in school. His only defense was, "You're telling a lie! I'm living with my mom and dad!" This case of teasing and lying demanded immediate action. David's fifth grade teacher said firmly, "We're not going to have any derogatory personal remarks about anyone in my class." He meant what he said and his pupils knew it. David wasn't bothered the rest of the day.

That night after school, the teacher asked David to help him clean the blackboard. He said, "David, you weren't telling the truth today All the class knew you were telling a lie, and I knew it. However, I can understand your reasons for lying. You aren't having an easy time of it, are you? Maybe I can help you; will you let me try?"

David nodded his head and then burst into tears. Giving the warmth of understanding the boy so desperately needed, the teacher patted the boy's shoulder. Later, he helped David look for techniques that would fit his personality and would protect him from his tormentors. These included:

a) Admit the truth and say, "Yes, I live with foster parents, and I like them."

b) Recognize that everyone has a right to keep silent about his personal business. In most instances, you do not have to go on the defensive. You don't have to answer questions.

c) When forced, develop such protective answers as, "I've been told not to say anything about that." Astute politicians have long adopted the "no comment" response to the reporter who attempts to corner and trap them into a defensive answer.

d) Avoid the tormenting situations before they occur. Do not allow yourself to get trapped. And when you are cornered, don't argue with others or accuse them of lying.

e) Learn to attract friends who like, support, and approve of you.

7. The "special case" who lies and cheats can best be handled by immediate attention and consistent control patterns. Use your counseling techniques to:

a) Terminate the symptoms of lying and cheating by getting at their immediate and obvious cause.

b) Help your "special case" recognize that you understand his actions, even if you do not condone them.

c) Let him know that you accept him as a human being.

d) Help him accept himself, and the reality of the situation as it exists.

e) Assist him in replacing the inadequate or socially unacceptable patterns he has been using in his interpersonal relationships with peers, inferiors, and superiors.

In dealing with liars and little cheaters at the elementary school level, immediate consistent discipline, coupled with well thought out and carefully implemented counseling will be your most effective tools.

A system of punishment and reward is always necessary. However, the balance should be weighted toward the side of reward. Too severe punitive action may tend to increase behavior problems. To be really successful, the "special case" must perceive positive benefits to himself, before he will change his present patterns.

Even under the most favorable conditions, it may be impossible to control your "special case." Time restrictions and your own personal emotional limitations must be considered. Referral may be the only course of action left open to you. The classroom learning situation, in view of the entire class's needs, must be maintained.

The fact that you are unable to resolve the "special case" problem may be the first indicator that a seriously disturbed child is in need of professional help. Don't hesitate to bring this case to the attention of your administration for possible referral to your special services department.

16

Appropriators and Little Stealers

The difference between borrowing and stealing is often a matter of maturity.

To the baby, everything in sight belongs to him. This is natural. The concept of ownership and property rights is a relatively mature one. Even in our adult society, there are many variations as to whether something is really stolen, found, borrowed, or simply acquired.

We have a saying, "Finders keepers, losers weepers!" It is an obvious invitation to steal anything which is not attached to its owner. As an example, American servicemen have been notorious for their "moonlight requisitioning." All merchants have a continuous problem of thievery. This arises not only from customers, but also from employees, many of whom feel they have some sort of inherent right to what they can take.

Social custom plays a large part in concepts of stealing. On the one hand, it would appear that in our society today, minimal penalties are paid for stealing inexpensive items or rather valuable property. For instance, a child who steals a stick of candy from a store will not be punished harshly. The bank president, if convicted of embezzling a large amount of money, will not be punished —on a proportionate basis—as severely as the man who steals an automobile or a few head of cattle—while the theft of a horse in a frontier economy, where survival depends on that animal, might be punishable by death.

Punishment and penalties are dependent on four factors:

  • The age and maturity level of the individual who steals.

150

- His reasoning power and capacity to know right from wrong.
- The value of what is stolen.
- Local customs and how they are applied to various forms of theft.

The baby has little sense of value. Whether he really wants it or not, he takes whatever catches his fancy. With maturity, his concepts change. How much they change may depend upon his training at home, the society in which he lives, his innate drives, and the development of his own personality.

The pre-school child is concerned largely with tangible objects. With maturity, he may reach out more and more for intangibles, provided they have value to him.

Penalties and rewards are prime teachers. Any child learns to steal or to refrain from stealing depending upon many stimuli that are constantly reinforced. On the one hand, punishment may teach him to refrain from taking what does not belong to him. He may also be rewarded by those around him for being honest. He may value the fact that his personal possessions are likewise protected by this same system and thus he supports the system. On the other hand, he learns to steal if he can satisfy his needs, and still not pay too high a price in pain, ostracism, and/or deprivation. The rewards of his peer group, if they support stealing, may induce him to continue stealing.

By the time he reaches kindergarten, he has a well developed awareness of what belongs to him and what belongs to others. Normally, he will know what he is doing when he becomes an appropriator or stealer. He is satisfying one or more of many basic needs, often at a time of personal crisis. These needs may include:

- Ownership.
- Status.
- To take for "taking's" sake.
- To "show off" and gain attention.
- To "put something over" on someone.
- To upset or worry someone—usually authority figures toward whom he is antagonistic—to release hostility.
- To buy love or provide self-love.

Therefore, a certain amount of stealing will take place in every elementary school; this is normal. In fact, almost every child will steal something and will probably be caught during this period of his life. Positive and appropriate action at this point by parents and teachers, or others in authority often is all that is needed for most children. Elementary school is the place to "corral" little appropriators and stealers. Stealing must be kept in check and line. Support your counseling by constant observation, confrontation, punishment, and group dynamics involving teachers, administration, and peers.

GUIDELINES TO CONTROL APPROPRIATING AND STEALING PATTERNS IN THE NORMAL CHILD

1. The needs to acquire possessions and to be thought important are basic. However, these needs must be fulfilled within acceptable channels, according to the age and culture of the group.

2. It is of utmost importance that appropriating, borrowing, and stealing be noted, and that the culprits be apprehended and dealt with immediately.

3. Be alert to the appearance of guilty looks and actions. Most children are poor liars. Without being mean, and with as much subtlety as possible, attempt to discover what is causing the feeling of guilt. Is it stealing?

4. Whether one or more children are involved, and the problem is appropriating, your best procedure is individual counseling. Many times the child is not really aware of what is happening and what the results of his actions may be.

5. Tattling, of course, will be a primary source of information. However, society looks askance at informers. Therefore, use tattling information with care. Often clues from tattling will enable you to uncover your own material. Rewarding informants is frequently disastrous to all concerned, and yet this source of knowledge should be kept open.

In addition, recognize that the tattletale, when he "spills the beans," is satisfying his own needs to control, to vent hostility, and to be important. Check all tales for validity.

6. There is always the possibility of a "plant" of stolen goods upon an innocent party.

7. Prompt, positive, and consistent punishment is urgent. The child who learns to "get away" with stealing will steal again. He develops a habit which is increasingly difficult to curb or to break.

8. Punishment must "fit the crime," as well as the age and maturation level of the child. Most children will respond to the concept that they will be punished if they continue to steal. They realize that their needs are better fulfilled by conforming to what society demands than by violating its rules.

9. As the child matures, you can appeal to his conscience, his intellect, and his desire to do right. In your counseling and in conjunction with the normal learning situation, discuss honesty, private property, and ownership rights. Let each child reason about what may happen to everyone involved if the pattern of thievery is not regulated.

10. Point out that, given the right opportunity, every child will occasionally steal. Stress the fact that all of us do wrong at some time, but that we must pay a personal and sometimes a public price for wrongs. Each of us has the capacity to learn and to change.

11. Strengthen a child's positive desire to do right, and to right the wrongs that he, as well as others, have done. Do this without reinforcing guilt feelings.

12. Delineate the occasion for stealing. Any normal child may become involved in stealing at a time of personal emotional crisis or of great personal need.

For example, a second grade student, Leonard, had been told to stay in his classroom during recess. This punishment occurred because he came late to school. Sitting alone at his desk, silently crying to himself, he saw an open box of candy on his teacher's desk. His self-pity and his need for self-love were so great that, almost subconsciously, he started eating the candy. Naturally, he was caught with a mouth full of chocolates. Intuitively, the teacher sensed his real needs, and thus understood his problem. She carried through a minimal punishment which involved a telephone call to the boy's mother in his presence. Then, she said emphatically, "Leonard, you'll not steal again, I'm sure. And I've talked to your mother. I realize it is not all your fault. Your mother will help you get to school on time."

This teacher had been perceptive enough to suspect that Leonard's problem was home-oriented. A later parent-teacher conference confirmed this fact. Leonard's mother was overworked and under much nervous tension, but she was cooperative. Leonard was not late again; nor did he appropriate further.

Thus, Leonard's teacher had accomplished three important goals:

- She controlled the immediate situation of appropriating.
- Possibly, she prevented future stealing by Leonard and his classmates.
- She supported Leonard by counseling with him and with his mother. Fortunately, the counseling occurred at a time of personal crisis, when both mother and child were endeavoring to satisfy basic needs.

EVALUATING THE COURSES OF ACTION

- Make the assumption that to a child there is a vast difference between appropriating and stealing. It is largely a matter of maturity, training, and conditioning through his interpersonal relationships and his environment.
- Be careful of your labeling. A few isolated incidents of stealing should not brand a child as a thief, a neurotic, or a psychotic—however, they are warning signals. Unless positive control and discipline are exercised, the child will experience greater and greater "need satisfaction" through stealing. At the same time, there occurs less and less ability to conform to society's standards.
- Do not condone appropriating and stealing. Minimize the rewards; maximize the hazards. Help each child reinforce his basic maturing needs, to weigh the social, moral, and legal consequences of his actions, and to accept the responsibility for these actions.
- Even if you consider the case normal, institute corrective action at once. Attempt to isolate the reasons, the motivations, and the drives which incite the child to appropriate or steal.
- Use checklists to aid you in determining whether a child is becoming a "special case" and needs your immediate additional help. Delay will only increase the complexity and severity of the problems whose symptoms surface in acts of appropriating and stealing

THE CHARACTERISTICS OF THE "SPECIAL CASE"

Because they are anti-social, as well as legally punishable, appropriating and stealing offenses must be faced immediately. If a child does not respond to normal discipline and control, he is a "special case."

What he steals is not nearly as important as the *fact* that he is stealing. Even more significant are his personality needs. Why must they be fulfilled by such acts?

Exercise firm disciplinary control. Consistent counseling must accompany this control so that the child will mature sufficiently to acquire a normal code of conduct.

Possibly no one person in the life of this "special case" is in a better position to help him more effectively than the teacher who has understanding, acceptance, and empathy.

GUIDELINES FOR PINPOINTING THE CHARACTERISTICS OF THE "SPECIAL CASE"

1. Never overlook an individual or a class problem of stealing. Is it spasmodic? Is it consistent?

2. Pinpoint who is actually stealing. Determine the circumstances. Is one person doing it? Is an organized group involved? Is the entire school having the same problem?

3. Understand that any type of recurring appropriating or stealing automatically categorizes the child as a "special case."

4. Attempt to determine whether stealing may be a symptom of a deeper-seated problem.

5. The stealing symptoms and syndrome may provide the initial clue to extensive emotional difficulties

6. Start your checklists by indicating whether the child is hostile, in need of love, seeking status, etc. Where possible, delineate the depth, breadth, and the intensity of such problems.

7. A characteristic of this as well as most "special cases" is that temptation is met in immature and unacceptable ways. In the same vein, the individual's code of conduct is relatively indefinite, ambivalent, and shifts from situation to situation.

8. A child will continuously test you and the system for which you stand. This testing increases in frequency and intensity as the severity of the "special case" increases. The "special cases" of appropriating and stealing will acquire great skill and stealth in controlling people and situations as he attempts to fulfill his needs.

When the problem is appropriating or stealing, don't minimize or delay your actions. The possibility always exists that the child may be developing extremely neurotic or psychotic tendencies and is in need of professional help.

DETERMINING TO WHAT EXTENT A CHILD IS BECOMING A "SPECIAL CASE"

Whether a little appropriator or stealer can be returned to normal or must be treated as a "special case," depends upon four factors.

1. Early detection of his appropriating or stealing.
2. Determination of the extent and depth of his problems.
3. Pinpointing the possible courses or needs that stimulated the child into adopting stealing symptoms.
4. How the problem is handled, disciplined, and controlled by the child, his peers, and superiors.

GUIDELINES IN DETERMINING WHETHER A "SPECIAL CASE" IS DEVELOPING

1. An isolated act of stealing may be regarded as normal. If the pattern repeats itself, the child must be considered immediately as a potential, if not an actual, "special case."

2. Discover whether the appropriating is simply for the sake of acquisition or status. Is there evidence that the stealing fulfills deeper needs? Is there a pattern of time, place, and situation? Daily stealing? Weekly? During recess? At lunchtime? On the playground? In the classroom? Going to and from school?

3. Are personal and school possessions disappearing? Are they returned? Is this done openly or surreptitiously? Who returns them?

4. Is the activity involving appropriating and stealing increasing? Change in the amount and frequency indicate the strong possibility of one or more "special cases." Does the activity appear to be impulsive, deliberate, or organized?

5. Is there a time and place relationship between the stealing and specific school, home, or community situations or events? Is there vandalism?

6. Does the possibility of a "plant" exist? What is the interpersonal relationship between individuals?

7. Is there tattling? Is it spontaneous? Is it solicited by you? Is it valid? Invalid? Exaggerated? Is there only one source? Several sources?

8. Determine whether the stealing is motivated by emotional needs, such as hostility toward society, a craving for love, or eagerness to be the center of attention. Pinpoint the reasoning behind the activity and the relationship between the individuals involved. Help the "special case" adopt other, more socially acceptable techniques for fulfilling his needs.

9. Normal discipline and supportive counseling should be effective in handling most problems of appropriating and stealing. When they are ineffective, or the situation is developing into a "special case," use checklists as a basis for determining what direction and what areas your counseling must cover to be effective.

10. Through your checklists, delineate the nature, extent, and progress of your "special case" situation. Always look for patterns in the symptom that may give you clues in understanding what is really happening.

HOW TO HANDLE THE CHILD WHO HAS BECOME A "SPECIAL CASE"

There are three courses of action open to you in helping the "special case" of appropriating and stealing:

1. Use a strict policy of rewards and punishments to accomplish your goals. The child will learn to:

- Control his stealing.
- Find other outlets that bring him greater rewards and fewer punishments.
- Learn to steal without getting caught.

2. Introduce him to the large part that social custom and interpersonal relationships play in concepts of stealing. Help him develop a personal moral code of conduct in keeping with his maturity level.

3. Take no action with the child.

The problem of stealing does not remain static. The child will either improve himself, or will deteriorate to the point where his case must be handled by school or community authorities.

Your checklists will provide you with specific notations. These will be helpful to you as you cope with the problem of helping your "special case." In addition, they will be important if you need to refer the child to your special services department or to school and community authorities. In addition, your checklists will guide you in determining the direction and the effectiveness of your counseling techniques.

GUIDELINES AS YOU COUNSEL THE
CHILD WHO HAS BECOME A "SPECIAL CASE"

1. Through direct and indirect counseling, show the difference between public and private ownership and usage.

For example, the chalk belongs to the school; it may be used here, but not taken outside or home. The water in the hall fountain is community owned, but free to the child. However, the contents of Jimmy's lunch box are privately owned and, tempting as they may be, are not to be taken without Jimmy's personal permission.

Concepts of private, public, or common ownership are difficult to grasp. As the child matures, he will face increasingly complex concepts of ownership.

2. Be aware that such things as "squatter's rights," "finders, keepers!" and "possession is nine-tenths of the law," do play a part in our society's views on appropriating and stealing.

3. Keep informed about the legal codes of your community and school system, and thus protect yourself as well as your pupils. Unfounded accusations of stealing can do grave, and possibly permanent harm to the innocent. Each child's reputation is very important to him and tends to shape his future. Often a child who earns a reputation as a thief, feels personally forced to maintain such a reputation because he has no face-saving "out."

4. Make maximum, but wise use of the feelings of guilt. They push an individual toward doing right. However, be well aware that indiscriminate use of guilt sets in motion destructive forces within a child's personality. A little guilt prods us to strive for the right, but too much makes us neurotic cripples.

5. Stress that even the small child, like the adult, must accept the responsibility of his own actions. Point out the price eventually paid for any type of stealing. Suggest other ways of meeting ownership needs.

6. Through verbalization and careful use of your checklists, examine the specific needs being fulfilled by the child's stealing. Cite them on your checklists. This will crystallize for you the importance of supporting the child in his search for more socially

acceptable ways to satisfy these needs. Frequently, you can see possible solutions he is unaware of. Your counseling will plant the seed and he will then discover the solution himself as he seeks to find appropriate need satisfaction.

7. Insofar as the child's capacities will permit you to do so, use reasoning and logic in your counseling. Acceptability is the key.

8. Help your "special case" recognize that when restitution has been made, his slate is clear. His stealing can be a thing of the past and need not be, like the Ancient Mariner's Albatross, a weight upon his soul. Too frequently, a very sensitive child is made to feel he hasn't been chastised enough. So he then continues to punish himself long after others have forgotten the incident By your actions and by your words, help him remove this useless albatross.

9. At least at the kindergarten and first grade level, it is easy to make games of returning the things appropriated during the day. This sets the stage for excellent learning situations and helps each child recognize his own possessions and those of others. Encourage the use of name places, tags, and other types of identification. Marked possessions are not often appropriated.

10. Aid the "special case" in learning to "make do" with what he has rather than to meet his needs by borrowing or appropriating.

11. If your "special case" has become a severe neurotic or psychotic, he must be referred for professional help.

12. When the little stealer's acts involve unacceptable sexual activity, such as stealing underclothing, and you feel uncomfortable in attempting to resolve the problem, consult your trained professionals.

Consistency on your part, regardless of what techniques you use, is the answer in controlling appropriators and little stealers. Be consistent with your discipline, support, solutions, your love, fairness, and your counseling.

17

Little Pugilists and Other Hostility-Venters

Restraint, frustration, and conformity generate hostility within the child. This hostility will be released, either in an acceptable or unacceptable way.

The drive to protect ourselves is instinctive. Any person or thing becomes our enemy when he, or it, threatens:

- Our well being.
- The satisfaction of our basic needs.
- The attainment of our individual goals.

Withdrawal and excessive attention getting, discussed in previous chapters, are two of many defense techniques we rely on to protect our personality.

Hostility is another. We release hostility, either toward a threat or toward a substitute of that threat. This defense may be either socially acceptable or unacceptable.

For example, a child may be very resentful toward his mother and/or father. He may express these feelings in many ways.

- He may exhibit them directly toward the parent.
- He may turn his hostility inward, thus hurting himself.
- He may transfer his resentment to the school environment, striking out at other authority figures.
- Afraid to strike back at a superior, he may strike out against, or hurt, individuals less able to protect themselves, such as smaller children.

160

- He may even hurt animals, or destroy inanimate objects.
Such hurtful and unacceptable actions may take many forms,
including:

- Pugilism.
- Cruelty.
- Rebellion against society, authority, and even himself.
- Antagonism against any type of law, order, and conformity.
- Self-punishment.
- Overt or covert hostile acts against any real or imagined
threats, or substitutes for these threats.
- Nagging, picking, complaining, and pecking.

Actually, all of these and related behavior patterns are com-
monplace and normal in the average elementary school. An unacceptable situation occurs when there is a steady increase in such
anti-social forms of hostility-venting, and where someone is hurt,
either physically or emotionally.

GUIDELINES TO CONTROL HOSTILITY-VENTING
IN THE NORMAL CHILD

1. Recognize that there is a continual need to release hostile
feelings. Help each child to do so in acceptable ways.

2. With understanding and empathy, give everyone some leeway
in "playing out," or expressing pent-up resentments. Even unacceptable ways of releasing hostility must be tolerated occasionally.

3. Be aware that the basic reason for each child's hostility is that
he is being forced to conform to home and school restrictions.
Much of his time and energy is expended in being "shaped-up"
to society's rules. This includes the society of his peers, as well as
of his seniors.

4. Develop a consistent pattern of adherence to the regulations.
You may say, "Regardless of what we are doing, we will always
begin and end recess with the bell. I feel that it is important to
keep to our school schedule."

Nothing builds up resentment more quickly than a feeling that
you "can't count on authority." If recess is frequently allowed to
extend overtime, every child is going to continuously test the
teacher and the administration to lengthen that time. No matter
how valid the teacher's changing decisions may be, each child is
resentful of inconsistency.

"Do what I do" is more effective than "do what I say." This is true for each of us, but is especially valid in the formative years of elementary school. Your leadership in following school rules will aid the child in making a right choice between conforming and rebelling.

5. Every child's background is different. If he comes from an environment in which extreme physical release is sanctioned, there will be within him a great drive toward pugilism. For the child's own well being, and that of the classroom situation, steer him toward acceptable release through supervised athletics.

6. In the same vein, abusive verbal release of hostility is even more common. The child accustomed to it will not hesitate to adopt it. As with physical hostility, the release of verbal hostility must be channeled.

Verbal animosity is dissipated easily through debate techniques, limited free-discussion periods, and the "give and take" of peer sharing groups. Release of aggressive feelings through political and other "cracker barrel" discussion activities has always been highly acceptable in the American way of life.

7. You cannot change the child's environment at home or in his special community. You can, however, be effective in improving his overall outlook. You can assist him in acquiring a realistic set of goals for survival in his society. Under no circumstances depreciate his family.

8. Regard closely a child's expressions of resentment and techniques or retaliation. Timely counseling may enable him to become aware of the sources of his resentment. He may then, at his own maturity level, be able to cope with and release them acceptably.

9. "A stitch in time saves nine" applies to fear, hate, and revenge, as well as to sewing. Early recognition of the problem and immediate action on your part may save you considerable time at a later date.

10. One "special case" of hostility endangers the whole class. Everyone may be injured. Self-preservation almost requires that each strike back in one way or another to protect himself. As the level and intensity of the striking back increases, learning decreases, and other class problems get out of hand.

11. A child's hostility will tend to bring to the surface your own normal hostility. If counseling is to be a part of your solution, schedule it when you are the least emotionally involved. There is

a tendency to over-react when we are mad and personally relating. Therefore, when you administer discipline and/or counsel your students, as far as is possible, be in control of yourself and of the situation.

A cooling-off period is always essential in any counseling. One needs some distance from the heat of the encounter to analyze the picture clearly, as well as to get the facts and feelings of all concerned. A delay until everyone simmers down is especially effective in counseling with little pugilists and other hostility-venters.

12. Hostile outbursts must be coped with. Each child needs to learn to recognize when he or one of his peers is "getting mad." As we mature, we learn what personal, peer, or authority controls are effective for ourselves as well as for others. For instance, a child cannot be allowed to pick up a rock and indiscriminately throw it, either offensively or defensively. Control by some source is imperative.

13. Attempt to pinpoint the specific causes when more than normal resentment is exhibited. Our level of hostility is affected by almost everything around us. This is as varied as what we eat, the weather, peer demands, authority requirements, what we read, hear, and see, and our own individual frustrations. Help the child, and your class in general, through judicious use of individual and group counseling to change what can be changed, and to successfully contend with what cannot be changed.

14. Punishment must be used because of its immediate effectiveness. If the child is to mature, it is necessary to support him in delineating and successfully fulfilling his drives and needs. Your counseling, understanding, support, and patience will enable him to find acceptable ways to live with these drives and to meet his needs.

EVALUATING THE COURSES OF ACTION

• Accept occasional outbursts of hostility and resentment. These are to be expected from everyone. They are normal to every group in our society. This is especially true in times of emotional tension and severe pressure. For instance, it is well known that toward the end of the school year when everyone is tired, restless, and looking forward to vacation, the number and the extent of emotional displays of anger rises.

- Recognize that from the mental health point of view, every child needs to eliminate resentments as they occur. If kept pent-up, that is, held within, the unresolved tensions tend to eventually lead to some type of physical or emotional illness.

- Delineate hostility as it is brought to school, as it develops and is expressed in the classroom and on the playground. Is it socially acceptable or unacceptable? As far as the individual is concerned, is it being used constructively or destructively? As far as the group is concerned? As far as you and the administration are concerned?

- Decide for yourself whether you personally bring out hostility in others. If so, attempt to discover the needs you are fulfilling. Substitute other outlets and ways to vent your own resentments. Channel them outside the classroom and school grounds, where students and faculty members are not involved.

Hard physical play or work is an excellent outlet. Verbal release may best be found outside of your professional environment. Adequate rest, change of pace, a consistent program of socializing with people who are not "school-oriented" will help you gain and maintain perspective. Participation in activities that involve and accept arguments, such as politics, is often very emotionally satisfying.

- Do not jump to conclusions. The problem of hostility is complex, fluctuating, and ever-increasing in our society.

As urbanization increases, frustrations increase. Hostility goes up and the need for adequate releases continually grows. Your students reflect this increase in tensions. Use your checklists to aid you in:

    a) Pinpointing the "special case."

    b) Determining the extent of the problem.

    c) Planning what action you may follow in helping the child.

    d) Resolving the problem as far as the "special case," the classroom, and the school are concerned.

THE CHARACTERISTICS OF THE "SPECIAL CASE"

The moment that unacceptable hostility "rears its ugly head," you have a potential "special case." Floyd, advanced for his age, has always displayed model deportment. He has pleased his teachers by being cooperative and by being an exemplary student. His fifth grade teacher, Mr. Frank Z., cannot believe the evidence when he sees Floyd and two of his classmates forcefully tearing the pants and underclothes from a third grade boy. Mistakenly, Mr. Z. blames the other boys. Actually, Floyd's participation makes him as guilty as the other two, and he is, at least at this point, a "special case."

The discipline and counseling procedures Mr. Z. uses with Floyd may be different than he uses with the other two boys. However, positive action is still called for because Floyd's release of hostility is completely socially unacceptable. He is physically and emotionally hurting others.

Behavior problems of unacceptable hostility must be faced immediately; treat each child as a "special case."

GUIDELINES FOR PINPOINTING THE CHARACTERISTICS OF THE "SPECIAL CASE"

1. Be attuned to the frequency, the extent, and the depth of hostility in your classroom and playground situations.
2. Watch for the manner and mode in which hostility is either released, or held within each child.
3. When you suspect that the releases are not normal, pinpoint the child immediately as a potential "special case."
4. Couple your empirical evaluation with specific observations. Determine whether the length, depth, and frequency of hostility are:

- Increasing.
- Decreasing.
- Fluctuating.
- Unchanging.

Hostility is broad. There are many varied and subtle ways in which it may be released or expressed. Your "special case" may adopt one, or several, anti-social techniques for expressing hostility and resentment. Some may be easily detected because they are active and outgoing. Others may be hidden, passive, and difficult to discern. Watch for the following:

- Pugilism and violence.
- Cruelty.
- Rebellion.
- Vandalism.

- Self-punishment.
- Acts to get others into trouble.
- Nagging, picking, complaining, and enforcing a "pecking order"—that is, who is number one, number two, number three, etc., in the class.

5. Physical violence is an indicator of a "special case." Although it is perfectly normal for an elementary school child to want to engage in pugilistic activity, it must take place in socially acceptable ways, such as in a supervised athletic program.

6. Evidence of cruelty denotes a "special case." The normal, and well-loved child is not cruel. He tends to like everything around him. But the child, as does the adult, adopts cruel patterns when others are cruel to him. As an aside, history is full of examples of oppressed peoples who have relieved their inner resentment against the cruelties of their environment and masters through outlets, such as bear-baiting, bullfighting, and fighting among slaves or professional gladiators.

7. Every child demonstrates some rebellion against conformity. But the "special case" tends to rebel almost continuously, using whatever pressures or tools are available to him. He tries to use everyone around him. He attempts to divide authority. He may use positive force or subtle maneuver to gain his ends. Pressuring you to violate the rules of your administration would be an excellent example. Often such pressures are so subtle and presented in such an unobtrusive way, that you, the recipient, are unaware of what is going on until you are committed or caught.

8. Vandalism, wanton mutilation, and destruction indicate a "special case." Pent-up feelings released by destroying property, whether it belongs to the child himself, to a peer, to the school, or to the community, is an unacceptable release of hostility. It is an indicator that something is drastically wrong.

An individual carving on a desk is just as surely engaged in vandalism as is a group destructively breaking into the school. Both require positive immediate action from authority figures.

9. Hostility often is released through self-punishment. The "special case" may:

    a) Refuse to cooperate or carry out an assignment for no other reason than the fact that he will be physically or verbally punished.

    b) Become a continuous pest, so that his needs for attention, etc., will be met through punishment by authority.

    c) Even engage in self-mutilation, such as cutting, scratching, digging, and picking his body. Hangnail and fingernail biting, scratching areas of the body until sores develop or are unable to heal, and cutting one's self with a penknife are outlets for hostile self-mutilation.

    d) Develop accident-prone behavior patterns that result in a relatively continuous occurrence of personal hurt.

If these tendencies recur so that a pattern develops, a child must be pinpointed as a "special case."

10. One characteristic of a "special case," and quite closely related to cruelty, is the derivation of pleasure from the pain and misfortune of others. Although he does not perform the act causing the disturbance, he literally "sets it up." This child enjoys getting those around him into trouble. When a "special case" exhibits such tendencies, the retaliatory hostility of those around him will increase. If unresolved, this "special case" may conceivably play:

- One child or a group against another.
- His family members against each other.
- One teacher against another.
- You against his family.
- His family against you and your administration.

11. Nagging, picking, complaining, and excessive pushing to establish a "pecking order" are all symptoms of the release of hostility. Carried to an extreme, the individual using them becomes a "special case."

Every teacher, unless she is especially fortunate, can anticipate one or more "special cases" of hostility in each class. However, excessive hostility cannot be tolerated if the school learning situation is to remain favorable. The "special case" must be identified. Positive action on your part and on that of your administration is vital. Discipline, using punishments and rewards, is the most frequently applied technique for terminating a specific hostile act. Discipline should be immediate and consistent. Counseling, both direct and indirect, should come later. It will enable the child to mature and to recognize what he is doing. This support helps him develop more acceptable patterns for the release of his pent-up hostility.

DETERMINING TO WHAT EXTENT
THE CHILD IS BECOMING A "SPECIAL CASE"

Basically, most societies are hostile. The continuous release of hostility is normal. How it is released, where it is released, and in what way it is released, are crucial factors. In the elementary school situation, these releases need to be socially acceptable and in accordance with the maturity level of the child. When they are not, a serious problem exists. Every child involved in this problem is handled as a "special case.' Use these guidelines:

• Be alert for the hostility syndrome. Determine what triggers it. Who is involved? What is the extent of the involvement? Does it include one or more individuals?

• Note the techniques used in release of hostility. Are these socially acceptable? Are the patterns of frequency, extent, and depth increasing, decreasing, or fluctuating?

• Do the problems involving hostility-venting shift from person to person, or from group to group?

• Through verbalization and observation, determine where the hostility originates. Is it internal, i.e. within the child? External? Generated in the school situation? Relatively unrelated to school? For example, if a child's parents are acutely hostile toward each other, those round them, and life in general, the child is going to learn his patterns of hostile release from them. To the child, it is a way of life and until he observes others who are not hostile, he knows no other way to act.

• Where does the problem appear to originate? At school? On the playground? In class? Before school starts? In one section of the room or schoolyard?

• From your empirical evaluation, attempt to discern whether the hostility is based upon real needs or whether the child is fantasizing. The excessive amount of hostility portrayed on television is easily adopted by the child.

• In what forms or ways is hostility released or expressed? Outbursts? Subtle jokes? Continuous hostile atmosphere? Overt or covert expression, such as direct confrontations or sullen undertones? Do the hostile acts involve pugilism? Violence? Cruelty? Rebellion? Vandalism? Self-punishment? Getting others into trouble? Nagging? Picking? Complaining? Enforcing a "pecking order?"

• Ascertain whether emotional, physical, and/or intellectual capabilities and limitations may be factors. Is anyone being hurt emotionally, physically, or intellectually? If so, who? By what techniques? In what way?

• Is the hostility acceptable in any way? Is it at times used constructively or only destructively, as far as the individual, his family, inferiors, peers, superiors, school, and society are concerned?

• Determine whether the action and counseling necessary to resolve the problem and to control the "special case" can be taken in the classroom or in the playground situation.

Use your checklists to determine the severity of your "special case," and to determine your line of approach in handling your pugilist and little hostility-venter. Time is important. Do not delay in involving your administration, and in taking positive action.

HOW TO HANDLE THE CHILD WHO HAS BECOME A "SPECIAL CASE"

As you institute positive action toward handling the hostile child who has become a "special case," two basic courses of action may be followed. Both have many variations.

1. You cope with the "special case" in your classroom and on the playground. You exercise control over the ways and areas hostility may be released by the class in general, as well as by the "special case." You help your "special case" live with the situations producing his hostility. At the same time, you help him develop socially acceptable techniques to release his hostility and improve his behavior patterns.

2. You postpone any action other than discipline, until the "special case" situation is out of hand; at which time, you refer the "special case" to your administration for disposition and resolution.

GUIDELINES AS YOU COUNSEL THE CHILD WHO HAS BECOME A "SPECIAL CASE"

1. "Special case" hostility in any form, whether pugilistic, verbal, or even quietly subtle, contains the seeds for anti-social and destructive behavior patterns. Cope with it immediately.

2. Discipline is always your first means of controlling hostility. However, by the time a child is a "special case," discipline of and

by itself, without counseling, will probably not be too effective.

3. Be aware that in some homes, physical fighting is the rule. Steve comes from such a family. His older brother pummels him constantly. At school, Steve's usual release is to "sock" anyone who disagrees with him. He tends to select friends who follow this same pattern. It is perfectly normal for Steve to fight. However, the smaller children can't take his hostility. For those who disagree with him, of course, he is turning to the famous last resort of any problem; and just as nations go to war; Steve "slugs it out." Both are concerned with the "balance of power." A weak nation seldom attacks a world power; a weak child seldom attacks a stronger one.

Your specific solutions for this pugilistic child are to:

a) Help him to "sock" those who can protect themselves, and allow him to do so only in organized athletics.

b) Teach him to release his hostility by "socking" acceptable inanimate objects, as in hitting baseballs, smashing at a tether ball, or even kicking the tin cans in a back lot where no one can be hurt.

c) Assist him in developing protective techniques so that he can either defend himself adequately, or avoid being pummeled by his brothers and others.

4 Whether the "special case" is in kindergarten or in sixth grade, your counseling techniques will be relatively the same.

5: Attempt to discover what is creating the excessive hostility. Help the child talk specifically about his hostile feelings and acts. Verbalize with him about such possibilities as: Does this hostility perhaps originate at home? Is someone in the class picking on him? Does he understand the class work? Can he see everything on the blackboard? What does he feel generates his hostile behavior patterns? Does he think he can release his resentments in more socially acceptable ways? How?

6. Is the child's hostility realistic or is it a result of fantasy? Physical, mental, or emotional imbalance?

Always be alert to the fact that you are the teacher, and not a professional psychologist. Make notes of what you do and the results of your actions. Do not make a specific diagnosis, but use your findings as the basis for your own counseling and for referral if professional testing and help are required.

7. Through group, as well as individual discussion, help the

"special case" be aware that everyone experiences hostile feelings and must cope with them.

8. Take advantage of hostile outbursts when they occur. They are normal. We all have them, but the "special case" has them more frequently and they are under less control. They provide perfect learning examples.

When Susie screams, "I hate you!" you can immediately and unemotionally reply, "Susie, we don't scream about hate, whether in the classroom or on the playground. Why are you so mad?"

The problem is simple if she says, "Julie pinched me." This can be handled by instant discipline. However, the problem is more complex if she really hates herself, authority, or those around her. Verbalizing alone may not solve Susie's problem. It does, nevertheless, allow Susie to ventilate her feelings and may provide her, as well as you, with helpful clues and insight. It also relieves pressure under which she is struggling. When Susie returns to a calmer state, she may be more amenable to your counseling. This is true especially as she becomes aware of the crisis she has undergone.

9. Through discussion and class programming, help the "special case" find socially acceptable ways to release pent-up frustrations. Role-playing is often an effective technique. In addition, you can foster:

   a) Physical outlets under supervision and with strict rules and regulations. For example, a child needs to yell "Kill the umpire" just as frequently as does an adult.
   b) Competitive sports.
   c) Classroom presentations such as debates, spelling bees, and sharing time in which resentments may be verbalized in controlled situations.
   d) Frequent discussions on why we have rules and why conformity is important. For example, "I know you'd like to come to school an hour early, Keith, but you just cannot. The lack of supervision and the school's responsibility for your safety require that you arrive and leave at a certain time. How do you feel about it, Keith? Are there any other possibilities with which I can help you?"

10. Use every opportunity for individual or group counseling to stress personal growth and mature ways of handling hostility. Complaint, like freedom of speech itself, should carry responsibilities as well as privileges.

11. Use the peer group, both in the classroom and on the playground, to help your "special case":

- Cope with his hostile behavior.
- Recognize that his hostility drives others away from him.
- Accept the fact that it is necessary for him to participate in the normal "give and take" of school life.

12. Even though a "special case" is young and immature, insight is always possible. As you utilize your counseling techniques and your classroom and playground learning situations, he can get an appreciation for our system of rewards for conformity, and penalties for non-conformity.

There is a little of the pugilist in each of us. Regardless of our ages, social or cultural backgrounds, hostility is always present. We learn to handle it, or it handles us! Pugilism, hostile acts, nagging, picking, complaining, and "pecking order," are all a part of our life.

You, the teacher, can help your little pugilists and other hostility-venters to be aware of their feelings and to express them in the most mature and socially acceptable ways possible.

18

Mavericks and Little Nonconformists

Maturity is the acceptance of some measure of conformity, responsibility, and authority.

Every species appears to have within its ranks the occasional exception to the pack, herd, or family. The rogue elephant, the lone wolf, and the man-eating tiger are the rebels, the "loners," the mavericks, and the complete nonconformists.

With Homo sapiens, it is no different. All societies of man have had to contend with the individual who is impervious or completely unresponsive to the accepted patterns of control and regulation of the group.

For most societies the solution to the problem of the "loner" or the nonconformist has been simple: eliminate him. He became the sacrifice to the gods, the slave, the inmate of whatever penal system existed, or simply the political or social prisoner who was banished or executed by those in power.

Our American society has been somewhat the exception. We have taken pride in allowing free thinkers and nonconformists as much leeway as possible. Partially because of encouragement to this type of individualism and to the freedom of action given him, the United States was colonized, developed, and became a world power.

The little nonconformist appears frequently in the elementary school. The needs of this child are usually great. His defenses tend to keep interpersonal relationships from developing. He may have one or more of the emotional problems discussed in this book. In

173

spite of your best efforts, he still may not respond to your teaching, counseling, and class-control techniques.

You must anticipate that at one time or another this child's problems will be severe enough that you will be called upon to guide and counsel him. He tends to respond poorly or not at all to discipline, social pressures from peers, and authority. He seldom reacts in the same manner as his classmates. He will frequently be the individual with a recognizable outstanding potential, both as a student and as a citizen. He also has the capacity to become an uncontrollable antagonist. If this occurs, society may be forced to protect itself by isolating him completely.

GUIDELINES TO CONTROL NONCONFORMING PATTERNS IN THE NORMAL CHILD

1. Each of us has a need to be an individualist and nonconformist once in a while. Taking such drives into account, you still must recognize and guide each child who has more than normal needs to be such a maverick. When it comes to fulfilling needs, there is a fine line between what action can be accepted in the school situation, what action should be slightly curtailed or changed, and what action must be terminated.

As a guideline in deciding whether control and counseling should be exercised, ask yourself, "Is this child, a peer, an authority figure, a junior, his family, or society in general being hurt in any way? Inconvenienced perhaps, annoyed, or put out, but actually hurt?" If "hurt" is involved, immediate action is probably called for on your part. If no one is being hurt emotionally, mentally, or physically, go slowly in any procedure you choose to take.

2. The need to be different is important to every child. Recognize, accept, and fulfill these needs. Yet each and every solution must be accomplished in personally and socially acceptable ways within the framework of society.

3. Likewise, the need to conform is extremely important to every child. Within each of us there is a constant struggle between this need to conform and to be accepted, and the need to be different— to be an individual and to make a unique contribution.

Donald M., a fifth grader from a middle class family in a small, west-coast city, demanded that his mother buy him blue jeans for school. He rebelled at having his jeans washed. Don wanted dirty blue jeans to conform to his peer group. He insisted, however, on a clean and vividly colored shirt every day. His shirt emphasized his individuality, it set him apart. The dirty jeans reinforced his membership in his peer group, Don's daily attire did not coincide with his mother's concept of suitable school clothing. However, she could accept his decision with the understanding that the jeans be washed, at least periodically. Actually, from every point of view, this solution was satisfactory. Don fulfilled his need in a pattern that was relatively, socially acceptable to his peers, his parent, and his school.

4. Punishment will probably be ineffective in many cases. In fact, punishment may well result either in repressing the symptoms that fulfill the child's need, or in his adopting another and possibly more unacceptable outlet. Such would be true where punishment establishes a negative pattern in the child that results in satisfaction through pain.

5. Direct and nondirect counseling is effective if it is structured to help the child recognize and accept:

- What he is doing.
- Why he needs to do it.
- Other possible solutions.

Your counseling may be done in a face-to-face relationship. It may also take the form of subtle interjections in the course of joint activities when ideas and concepts are shared—as you, the teacher, and your student or students become involved in learning situations. Or as is frequently the case, your counseling may be a combination of both techniques.

6. As the child matures, his capability of accepting and utilizing insights into his behavior patterns increases. Because of a necessity to protect his psyche and an inability to adjust, he may tend to become more of a rebel or nonconformist. On the other hand, and this tends to be the usual growth pattern, he may, through his own insights and the support of others, develop relatively acceptable behavior patterns that minimize his anti-social, harmful, or negative actions.

EVALUATING THE COURSES OF ACTION

1. The little nonconformist often meets the stresses, strains, and confrontations of his life quite differently from that of the normal

child. His solutions and defenses are inclined to be unique. Although he may be thought of as somewhat of an introvert, this is not always the case. Just because he is different does not mean that he cannot effectively exist in his society. Accept him. Help him understand himself and recognize what is happening in his interpersonal relationships with those around him. Your evaluations should establish the fact that he is a little maverick and that his nonconformity is creating trouble that either he or those around him cannot effectively handle.

2. In general, positive controls, discipline, and restrictions are relatively ineffective with this type of child. Since his solutions may be bizarre or of a type that are entirely unexpected or unpredictable, your courses of action in living with, counseling, and producing the most meaningful climate must be "played by ear." Your techniques will flex to suit the immediate situation. Your personal warmth and understanding are essential. Trial and error, coupled with your previous experience, will be your best method of learning how to help this child adopt more socially acceptable defense techniques.

3. The neurotic personality of the "loner" is so often pictured in the fiction and fantasy world of television, movies, and novels as a lovable, poorly understood, but "salt of the earth" character. This certainly is not true in the reality of the school and playground environment where cooperation and teamwork are so important. He is usually hard to draw out and help. He may be rebellious and sullen. He may be quiet and refuse to communicate, isolating himself until he is ready to act. Often he becomes the one picked on by the group. In and out of school, and in many areas, such as discipline, communication, learning, group participation, and group control, he frequently is a continuing problem for the teacher.

4. In considering your courses of action, it is wise to remember that from the mavericks and nonconformists have come many of the great inventors, discoverers, and independent thinkers that the world has produced. This child may be one with great potential. Your understanding counsel may guide him to develop his special talents, satisfy his specific desires and needs, and at the same time, help him conform to the restrictions and controls of his society and of his school environment.

5. Be slow to label or pinpoint this child as a "special case." Use your checklists to determine the directions his actions and personality traits take. When the need appears, supply the additional sup-

port and counseling. Record what you have attempted to do and the results, if any.

THE CHARACTERISTICS OF THE "SPECIAL CASE"

If you, the elementary school teacher, suspect that you have a normal child who is becoming the "special case" of a maverick or a little nonconformist, move slowly. Before classifying him as a "special case," give yourself and your administration ample time. Wait until you have evaluated your checklists and carefully noted your observations.

Unlike many "special cases" discussed in this book, that of the "loner" or the nonconformist usually does not demand an urgent response from you. In many instances this child may be creating only a minimal disturbance to the school and learning situation. He may be causing little or no harm to others. In cases where actual physical, mental, or emotional harm is occurring, immediate positive action is mandatory. The specific actions involving hurt may be stopped at once, but the eventual solution of the child's problem will be more difficult.

Discipline, normal rewards, and the subtle or forceful pressures that spur most children, seldom do little more than create resistance and additional nonconformity with this child.

A characeristic of this "special case" that is so difficult for the conscientious teacher to live with is that very few recognizable indicators may appear that delineate the progress or success that you, the teacher, are achieving. Even when your counseling is making continuing progress, the child's defenses may be so well developed and his ability to keep his feelings and reactions to himself so effective, that your efforts seem almost completely wasted. Your direct indication of any success may be in the form of a long delayed and unsuspected breakthrough. It may be revealed to you in a very minor comment from the child himself, or from a remark made by someone else who has observed him closely.

Donald was a little rebel and nonconformer in Miss Jones's third grade class. He came from an underprivileged background, was relatively intelligent, but quite unproductive in class. He seldom "out and out" refused to do what was requested of him. However, when asked, Donald invariably did either something else or nothing at all. He got up and walked around when he wanted to, or proceeded on his own projects. Frequently, Donald would accomplish a task assigned to every member of the class. Nevertheless, he would proceed by an entirely different and unprescribed route, and at his own rate of speed. Neither his teacher nor his peers seemed to influence his actions. He accepted praise, but it did not spur him on to greater cooperative efforts. In the same vein, he accepted punishment and authorities' displeasure. It neither curtailed nor changed his behavior patterns.

Although Miss Jones and her two predecessors had tried, no one had succeeded in helping Donald fit successfully into the learning and maturing pattern of his group. Class projects, experiments involving raising animals (such as baby chicks), giving him leadership and roles of responsibility, compliments, and personal counseling, were all attempted without success.

Toward the end of the year, an event happened that initiated the breakthrough in helping Donald. A new boy, Carl, came into the class. Carl had attended five schools since kindergarten and had slowly developed his protective defenses to the point where, like Donald, he was a maverick. Both boys felt this kinship and were drawn to one another; Miss Jones sensed the potential of the relationship. It was her opportunity. Counseling at this point involved both boys. Slowly, the interpersonal relationships of Donald and Carl began to include their peers.

With little nonconformists, it is difficult to find the combination for success. After you pinpoint and delineate the characteristics of this "special case," proceed slowly, but do not give up. Success may be at a "snail's pace" in coming, but there is no relatively easy way.

GUIDELINES FOR PINPOINTING THE CHARACTERISTICS OF THE "SPECIAL CASE"

• Recognize that being a maverick or a little nonconformist, at least to a certain point, is desired by many. It is pretty much an accepted and often admired trait in our society.

• Attempt to empirically evaluate from your observations and your checklists whether other emotional problems are involved. If they are, will their resolution, or at least their partial resolution, eliminate this child from the "special case" category?

• Just exactly how is he a maverick? Does he isolate himself?

Does he do the unexpected? Is his behavior bizarre? Does he change when others imitate him?

• Pinpoint whether the child actually refuses to conform regardless of the situation, or whether he conforms in certain instances, but not in others. What appears to evoke a response from him? How is it accomplished? By whom? In what situation?

• Pressure will usually increase his nonconformity. Discipline may have little or an undesired effect. His response to stimulus that encourages the normal child to participate, excel, or cooperate with seniors, peers, or juniors, will be at variance with, or in opposition to, what might be anticipated from other students. He may, in fact, exhibit no visible response at all.

• One of the characteristics of this "special case" is his seeming imperviousness to any type of attention, warmth, or understanding on the part of others.

The "special case" who is a little nonconformist may have developed many neurotic symptoms. He may, however, just as likely appear relatively well-adjusted to his society. If he is causing little disruption to those around him, accept him as he is. If a change is advisable for his own personal growth within his society, do not push. Be consistent. Work toward the long-term goal, striving for a little progress each week. Use only the most favorable conditions for your counseling.

DETERMINING TO WHAT EXTENT A CHILD IS BECOMING A "SPECIAL CASE"

Analyzing the extent of the problem of the "special case" who is a rebel, a "loner," or a general nonconformist, tends to be quite difficult. This "special case" is frequently pretty non-communicative. Unless his activities severely get in the way or impede the achievement of the goals of those around him, or unless someone is physically or perhaps emotionally hurt, the extent of the little nonconformist's behavior and problems are hard to determine.

In general, this "special case" will adopt definite techniques and defense patterns that will be evaluated by others in three ways:

1. Actively and violently he will be at odds with any rules, codes, or ways of accomplishing prescribed goals that are set up by authority or peers. Generally, he will make no

effort to hide his distaste for those who do what they are supposed to do or who cooperate with the group. Any act of punishment, derision, or pressure toward changing him merely strengthens his convictions and resolutions.

2. He may passively be at odds with society, rules, and conformity, but his behavior pattern will be quiet, covert, and relatively unobtrusive. He will just take a "steady strain" against everything. When forced, through severe pressure or punishment, he will go along with what is required, but he will not accept it. He will subtly attempt to sabotage and will detach himself from the distasteful situation at the first opportunity, and as inconspicuously as possible.

3. He may use a combination of both of the above. Here his actions are colored by the various individuals and the different situations that force him to conform.

GUIDELINES IN DETERMINING WHETHER A "SPECIAL CASE" IS DEVELOPING

1. Every child needs to rebel against the "rules" or the "establishment" once in a while. It helps in the maturing process. Each of us needs to know, "How far can I go in any situation before I am stopped?"

2. The child who is a periodic maverick or little nonconformist is not a "special case." Such behavior only becomes a severe problem if it increases in frequency, intensity, and depth to the extent that someone is being hurt. This "hurt" may be physical, or it may be an unseen hurt that results in the disruption of the child's learning and maturing.

3. Is there a specific and relatively definable pattern that his nonconformity takes? Is intellectual capacity, social and emotional maturity, or some physical anomaly contributing to the developing of his nonconformity? Is he liked, disliked, tolerated? By whom? Does he communicate with others? How? Is it adequate? Spotty? Poorly developed?

4. Determine, if possible, the reason for the rebel actions. Pinpoint the origin of the needs, drives, and fears that feed his actions. Do they originate within the child himself, or are they supplied by his home or the environment around him? Does he appear to be happy? Unhappy? Miserable? Who or what may be causing or in-

creasing the severity of his problem? Through direct and indirect counseling, attempt to ascertain, "Am I able to modify or change the actions, points of view, or interpersonal relationships that are a part of this 'special case'? "

Your careful notations on checklists will give you a visible tabulation as to whether:

- The behavior patterns of nonconformity are increasing or decreasing.
- They are creating problems in the learning situation.
- This "special case" reacts in specific or varying ways to your patterns or the patterns of others in the areas of discipline, persuasion, cooperation, personal warmth, and general counseling techniques.

HOW TO HANDLE THE CHILD WHO HAS BECOME A "SPECIAL CASE"

There are three courses of action available to you, the teacher, in working with the "special case" of the maverick and the little nonconformist:

- Accept him as a person and human being. Do no more for him than you do for any other child in your class. Unless the nonconforming "special case" is creating difficulties in the classroom or on the playground, this is generally the course of action adopted by most already overworked teachers.
- Consistently give him special warmth and support that will extend over a relatively long period of time. This attention, more than his contemporaries receive, is done without the use of any special counseling. It does, however, involve more understanding and a little extra consideration in the learning and playground situation. The hope is that this "extra" will give your "special case" the inner strength to begin to find himself and adjust to his environment in a more socially compatible and satisfactory way.
- In addition to warmth and support, use direct and indirect counseling, striving continuously to find the key to the combination of this particular "special case." You will find yourself going ninety percent of the way with this child in helping him to verbalize, play out his feelings, and gain insight into why he chooses the behavior patterns he does. Your counseling will involve helping him understand and accept his feelings. Such acceptance may not necessarily

mean that he will change appreciably. He still might decide that being a little nonconformist is the only way he can survive in the society in which he lives.

GUIDELINES AS YOU COUNSEL THE CHILD WHO HAS BECOME A "SPECIAL CASE"

1. Observe and talk with your "special case." Let him ventilate his feelings. Make careful notations on your checklists. Date these notations for future review. Your progress is easier to ascertain if your observations and results are carefully noted and dated.

2. Attempt to determine the possible causes of his anti-social behavior patterns. Why is it so necessary for him to be a "loner," a maverick, or a nonconformist? What needs are being satisfied?

3. As you pinpoint the suspected reasons, pressures, or needs that appear to trigger his specific behavior patterns, use direct and indirect individual counseling. Make an effort to help him open up and verbalize about his needs in relation to his behavior patterns. Always subtly interject the thought-provoking questions, "Is there another or perhaps different solution? How else can you satisfy your needs and attain your goals?"

4. Structure the class and playground situations in an attempt to place this "special case" in a position to develop better interpersonal relations with specific peers. Use those who may be able to draw him out, relate to him affirmatively, or support him in areas where his fears and resentments appear.

5. Allow him a time and place to rebel, to be a little nonconformist. Accept this. Then help him to use such opportunities as a means of learning how to fulfill his needs in more socially acceptable and perhaps more rewarding ways than he is presently using.

6. Give him support and warmth through verbalization, activities, and actions that strive to include him. Demonstrate the positive values our society places on conformity. What does success mean to him?

7. Frequently, this "special case" will have an above average intellect. Use it in helping him logically find solutions to more effective interpersonal relationships with those around him. Subtly and directly use such questioning techniques as: "How would you handle this problem if you were I?" "How could I, as your teacher,

utilize your abilities to help other members of this class?" "What would you like to do or learn that the others in the class are not able to do at this point, but that you are?" Attempt to put his etxra capacity to work in satisfying his own goals and drives, as well as helping you with less capable students.

8. In the same vein, this "special case" may be the low achiever or the below average ability student. Look for his special talent. Each of us has at least one area where we feel more secure and more successful. This is the starting point. I think that helping this child feel needed and a part of your learning program is the most essential element in overcoming his behavioral problem. Help him to talk to you. This is best done when he is with you alone, or with you and a small group of two or three others who are doing a special project. Listen. He will tell you, maybe very indirectly, but nevertheless he will tell you where and how you can reach him.

9. Patience, kindness, consideration, and tolerance toward his nonconformity are hard traits for any instructor to acquire. You must be consistent, and yet certain school standards are required. However, ample use of these traits with this "special case" tend to be extremely effective over an extended period of time.

10. This is the type of "special case" that responds well to rather lengthy periods of individual and personal companionship. As an example, if you are able to take a long walk with this child where you can communicate about many things, or participate with him in a lengthy session of music or art appreciation, your positive influence will increase. You may be able to get other members of his family, other school personnel, or even his peers to take time to use this same technique.

11. Keep precise records, dated and documented, with your observations and empirical evaluation. Included should be suggested techniques and plans of action for your counseling, determining which have been effective and which have not.

Do not expect immediate results or a rapidly improving situation with this "special case." Progress is always slow and is generally difficult to determine and measure. This is especially true in cases where communication is poor, or is distorted by different sets of fluctuating values. Semantics is always a problem in communication. This particular type of "special case" may take several years in its successful resolution. Your efforts and progress will be passed on to this child's next teacher, who may be the one to reap the results of your work. Your personal emotional reward, however, will be great.

As you deal with the behavioral problems in the elementary school, you will find that regardless of what type of "special case" is involved, one word is always associated with success—LOVE. It must be genuine. It must be consistent. The growth in stature and wisdom that can be accomplished through the understanding warmth of one human being for another is incomprehensible.

The race does not always go to the swift alone, but to the consistent, conscientious, and patient striver who sets a goal and plods toward this goal until success is attained.

APPENDIX

GUIDELINES FOR USING YOUR CHECKLISTS EFFECTIVELY

1. Pinpoint the problem child. Start the checklist to record his behavior patterns.

2. Watch the symptoms of the "special case." Does the child seek attention only during the first few minutes, or the first hour? Is there a frequency and a consistency which can be traced?

3. Do not make an issue of the problem so that the class becomes involved. They may take sides for or against you, or their classmate. This only creates additional class disturbances.

4. Do not allow the problem to become chronic. Give thought and consideration to the specific action you take. Beware of impulsive action.

5. Use your checklists to avoid becoming personally and emotionally involved.

6. Keep the checklists in a manner that will make them helpful if it becomes necessary to refer the "special case" for action by school administrators or outside professional help.

SAMPLE CHECKLISTS

The following sample checklists (I-VI) are designed to give you, the elementary school teacher, a basis for preparing your own evaluation criteria. They are not applicable to every "special case," nor are they complete in every detail. In actual use you will find yourself constantly revising (adding, eliminating, and supplementing) your own lists, so that they may become the core of your written records on a particular case.

I

Pinpointing and Determining Whether the Child is Becoming a "Special Case" of —————————

Date:	Yes or No	Not Apparent at this time
1. What symptom or symptoms are exhibited?		
2. Is the child possibly becoming a "special case" in more than one area?		
3. Is the entire class involved? A small group? Only one child?		
4. Where does it occur? Classroom? Playground? To and from school? At home?		
5. What is the frequency of occurrence? Is there a time pattern? What is the length of time involved in the behavior pattern?		
6. What types of patterns occur? Describe.		
7. What techniques are employed? Do they appear to be deliberate? Conscious? Subconscious? If not socially acceptable, are they socially allowable?		
8. Does support or pressure come from peers? Siblings? Mother? Father? Other adults? Groups, such as church? Scouts? Teams?		

Date:	Yes or No	Not Apparent at this time
9. Does he return to reality or normal activity by himself? Through pressure by others? Is this done with ease? With difficulty?		
10. What is the amount or extent of the disruption to the child? Class? Teacher? Administration? Others?		

Frequency, Duration, Intensity	Times of day and where acts occur	Needs further evaluation	Comments and evaluation	Plans of action, what has been effective and ineffective

II

Determining the Possible Pressures on and Tension within the Child Who is Becoming a "Special Case" of ————————.

Date:	Description	Comment
1. Have the pressures around him changed recently? At home? At school? In the community?		
2. Where do most of the pressures appear to originate?		
3. How are his tensions released? Is there thumbsucking and/or nailbiting? Drumming his fingers? Hitting? Running? Does he scratch himself? Does he abuse himself by hair-pulling, etc.? Does he engage in fighting?		
4. Are the pressures and tensions being reinforced by specific actions? Do these originate with the child? With his peers? With school authorities? With you, the teacher?		
5. Are the pressures and tensions real or imagined? Or a combination of both?		
6. Are the pressures increasing? Decreasing? Fluctuating? Remaining constant?		
7. Do they appear to be internal or external? Or a combination of both?		

Date:	Description	Comment
8. Does anything about this child—his home, his environment, or his own personality—indicate excessive unfulfilled physical, emotional, or mental needs?		
9. Do there appear to be nebulous, unfulfilled needs? Can you pinpoint them?		
10. Is there evidence of excessive and nebulous fears? Anxieties? Pressures? Tensions?		
11. Is a punishment syndrome involved? A pleasure from pain or hurt? Or a need for the attention that will be gotten through suffering?		
12. Does the problem appear to have been of long duration?		

III

Determining the Possible Causes of the Symptoms and Contributing Factors in Forcing the Child to Become a "Special Case" of ——————————— .

Date:	Yes, No, Possible, Undetermined	Comment
1. Is there a physical anomaly? Deformity? Is the child an early developer? Larger or smaller than peers?		
2. Is there a mental or learning problem? Too far above or below the group? Problems in one area of learning?		
3. Are there emotional instabilities?		
4. Is he aware of what he is doing? Completely? Partially? Not at all?		
5. Do the unacceptable behavior patterns appear at any specific time of day?		
6. Does the problem appear to be generated and fed by forces within the child?		
7. Is the child's behavior pattern affected by peer or authority relationships? Is he able to share? Is he a troublemaker? Does he need to win or succeed?		
8. Does the problem appear to originate at home? In the classroom? On the playground? On the way to and from school?		

Date:	Yes, No Possible, Undetermined	Comment
9. Does the child find it difficult to adjust to his environment? At home? At school? On the playground? With authority? With peers?		
10. Is there an interrelationship between the various factors involved in the problem?		
11. Is there a strong (defined or undefined) unfulfilled need?		
12. Are there immature patterns involving self-love?		
13. Does there appear to be a real need for self-punishment? Why? In what way?		
14. What personal drives, inadequacies, or other needs appear to be satisfied by his antisocialism?		
15. Does he appear to be a leader? A follower? A lone wolf?		
16. Does the child appear happy? Occasionally happy? Generally unhappy? Miserable?		

IV

Estimating Whether Physical and/or Emotional Problems Are a Factor or Contributing Factors Forcing the Child To Become a "Special Case" of ———————— .

Date:	Comment	Follow-up Evaluation
1. Smaller or larger than peers?		
2. Problem of age—younger or older than most?		
3. Visible physical loss, such as an arm, leg, hearing, sight, or other?		
4. Physical anomalies, such as red hair, freckles, eye color, scars, repaired cleft palate, etc.?		
5. Readily discernible difference involving speech, clothes, culture, religion, income, etc., from peer group?		
6. Is there a problem of maturation and puberty? (For example, only one girl in the class is developing breasts, and while she has no wish to attract attention, she may be receiving it from her peers.)		
7. Sexual variations, such as that of the only boy from an all girl family, or the only girl from a family of all boys. Such a child may demand excessive attention to develop rapport.		
8. Unusual family situation (death, divorce, temporary separation, parent hospitalized, severe accident or illness)?		

V

Evaluating the Development and the Extent of the Problem of a Child Who Has Become a "Special Case" of ————————.

Date:	Pertinent comments	Follow-up comments
1. Type of behavior. Primary symptoms? Secondary symptoms? Are additional symptoms appearing (physical, mental, emotional, etc.)? In what way?		
2. Frequency and duration of occurrence? Does it shift? Fall in a pattern? Short periods? Long periods?		
3. Who is involved? One? Two? Several? The entire class? Is the child liked? Disliked?		
4. Extent of involvement? Is it creating a problem for you? For the peer group? For the administration? Others?		
5. Ease with which involvement is initiated? Terminated?		
6. Who starts it? Ends it? Individual? Small group? The entire class? Is there a pattern of control?		
7. Means used in originating and terminating unacceptable behavior patterns. Where does the pattern occur? Classroom? Playground? On the way to or from school?		
8. Is the problem temporary? Chronic? Acute?		

Date:	Pertinent comments	Follow-up comments
9. Is there a history of medical or psychological involvements?		
10. Is there a history of physical, mental, or emotional problems?		
11. Are noticeable physical anomalies evident, as scars, bleeding, sores, or distortion of areas of the body?		

VI

Evaluating the Overall Status and Possible Disposition of the Child Who Has Become a "Special Case" of ——————————— .

Date:	Comment	Recommendation	Follow-up date	Disposition
1. Are the child's behavior patterns tolerable to the classroom? The child himself? His peers? The learning situation?				
2. Are the problems of this "special case" increasing? Decreasing? Remaining unchanged? Add pertinent information received from sources involved.				
3. Have all avenues of help within the classroom been exhausted? Is the child in need of referral?				
4. What courses of action have been taken? Are there others you haven't taken or do not wish to try at this point?				
5. How long have you been giving this "special case" specific consideration? Discipline? Counseling?				

Date:	Comment	Recommenda-tion	Follow-up date	Disposition
6. How much further time do you feel may be needed to achieve a relatively successful disposition?				
7. Do you feel that the child, as well as the entire class will profit by the removal of this "special case" from the normal classroom situation?				
8. What help has been sought from and what action taken by:				
a. Teacher (yourself)?				
b. Other teachers?				
c. Principal?				
d. School counselor?				
e. Nurse?				
f. Physician?				
g. Psychiatrist?				
h. Psychologist?				
i. Member of special service department?				
j. Priest? Rabbi? Minister?				
k. Civil authorities (government and private law enforcement)?				
l. Other agencies (public or private)?				

Date:	Comment	Recommendation	Follow-up date	Disposition
9. A chronological history of action taken and its effect.				
10. Medical and psychological history, if any. Is there a connection between findings recorded and the present behavior patterns? Diagnosis? Prognosis?				
11. What is your personal prognosis?				

Index